Heart-Led
Living

"*There are those who talk about the process of Individuation, and those who live it. What Cara Barker has achieved is a true realization of what it means to bring forward the essence of one's true life. Well-versed in the essence of transformative process, she is destined to become one of the Voices for the Seeker of their own Truth.*"

–Helen Luke, founder of Apple Farms, and author of *Woman: Earth and Spirit, The Way of Woman,* and *Kaleidoscope*

"*What a gift it is to have one's path cross with kin. When I first met Cara Barker several decades ago, during an interview, I was struck with her capacity to put her hand on the pulse of the moment in a way that left me feeling heard, comprehended, and held in love. She is truly Sophia's daughter . . . her work with the Sacred Feminine is what we need in this world, so overflowing with unexamined Darkness, and its consequences of pain. I am proud to call her a sister in our shared work as Jungian Analysts.*"

–Marion Woodman, Jungian Analyst and author of multiple works including: *Addiction to Perfection, The Pregnant Virgin, Leaving My Father's House, The Owl Was a Baker's Daughter, Coming Home*

"*There are those who are content to live inside the boundaries others set, and those who are compelled to become. It was clear to me from the very first meeting, that Cara is a global citizen, at home in the world, wherever she is. I consider her a sister to the Soul, a messenger for the times up ahead, a voice from the heart of one who has undergone the most difficult and used it as fodder for the mill of transformation, a giver of the gift most precious.*"

–Sir Laurens van der Post, author of the *The World of the Kalahari, A Far Off Place, The Heart of the Hunter, Feather Fall* among others. Godfather to King Charles, Sir Laurens was the first white man from South Africa to stand up against Apartheid.

The 4 Cornerstones to Building a Better Life

Heart-Led Living

CARA BARKER, PH.D.

Published by Best Seller Publishing
www.BestSellerPublishing.org

ISBN (paperback): 979-8-9904486-0-5
ISBN (ebook): 979-8-9904486-1-2

Book design and production by www.AuthorSuccess.com
Cover art by © Ledenev | Dreamstime.com

Printed in the United States of America

For you, the reader, as well as our children's children
May you know from your heart, that you need not
chase what you want to receive.
The trick is not striving, but living a guided life.

Contents

Introduction

For every successful new construction project, four cornerstones must be well placed. This is just as true for building your better life. I'm not saying 'perfect' life, as the newsstand headlines promise. I am saying that laying the correct, solid cornerstones for a re-envisioned, more meaningful life is required to create the outcome your heart desires. And even before laying the foundation, a sound blueprint must be in place.

While in an Army Nursing Program during the Vietnam War, I learned something that radically changed my life's direction. Maybe you, too, have had such a moment? For me, it was the discovery that *our deepest wounds are invisible.* As a trained Jungian psychoanalyst, I love working with the invisible to solve tangible, real-life problems that liberate the human Spirit.

The truth is that the deepest source of our suffering is unknown to us. While we might attribute our pain to a present event (such as heartbroken grief from child loss, depression, suicide of a loved one, or chronic and exhausting physical pain), trauma's unassimilated ancestry goes down to the deepest roots of our present pain. This is not to say pain is not real. It is real. But there's more to the story.

The following pages contain some of my own heart-centered Wisdom. Wisdom does not come from professional training (in my case sixteen years of clinical training), nor the fifty-four years I have spent assisting others in this arena. Head training and theory are all well and good, but they are not the complete answer.

Western culture promotes the lie that life should be comfortable. It isn't. To 'medicate' the disease, we are urged to go shopping, buy the latest detergent, shoes, Teslas, and programs that would change our discomfort into materialistic bliss.

We are also urged to have a purpose that is bigger than Broadway lights. It's tempting to believe that anything that counts in a life well-lived must be huge. It does not. This is unrealistic. Accept that we might not be able to change the world, but we can change the world of another, one person at a time.

What is required to do so is your willingness to commit to a daily practice of an appointment with your own heart. Commit to regarding yourself, and your issues, with deeper compassion every day.

You'll find exercises and writing prompts throughout this book that I call "prescriptions" to take you into heartful contemplation and discovery. Find your own supportive setting that encourages quietude, perhaps in a favorite chair, in nature, in the shower, in your car, wearing earphones, or whatever works in your life.

Developing an ear to the silent whisper of our heart takes simplifying; clearing away clutter, distractions, the phone, or whatever has the power to seduce our thoughts away from our heart.

Practice patience, allowing your heart-led conversations to develop over time, becoming more meaningful over time. You will benefit from the inspiration, validation, inclusion, companionship, and self-compassion that will result from this practice.

All it takes is slowing down, being present, simplifying our own life, and developing patience and compassion for yourself and others.

I do not know your Calling; your deepest longing, and maybe you aren't clear about what it is quite yet, either. Let's journey together in these pages to find your Heart-Led Life.

Cara Barker
January 2024

SECTION ONE

Your First Cornerstone: Digging and Clearing the Earth

Reviewing Your Story of You

Self-Quiz: So as not to waste your time, please circle what applies to you:

1. Have you been putting off something that would lift your Spirit?

2. Have you wished the craziness in this world would stop?

3. Are you concerned about the world we are leaving our children?

4. Have you had a hearty laugh yet today?

5. Have you ever wondered what your Purpose is in this life now?

6. Do you make it a daily practice to ignite your creative fire?

7. Do you ever wonder what is your best next step to create your best life?

8. Are you allowing toxic people into your space?

9. Does work seem like the 'same old, same old?'

10. Have you ever felt an inconsolable longing?

Hopefully, these markers will give you a picture of your present state: what's working well and what isn't. Keep in mind that fear is our biggest obstacle. I call fear the Great Predator, (although we each have our own garden variety). By way of an embarrassing example, during middle school, I was an approval suck. Oh, how I wanted to be loved, approved of, liked. And it was that, my dear reader, which led me further away from who I really am. Eventually I got sick of hiding.

I don't know if this is true for you, but in my neighborhood, bull-dozers are everywhere. The same thing is true wherever I go. But in ours, eight sweet little cottages that were built in the 1940s have been trashed. Especially fond of them, one day, I was told that four of them were owned by a frail man who had survived the Holocaust. Shortly thereafter, the ninety-four-year-old owner died. As fast as it takes to blow out a candle, realtors and land development men were all over the street. Like lightning, all the unique creativity that built humble charm was no more. In their place are now sixteen townhouses that look like bland shoeboxes for boots. No earth for gardens remains, only a few feet between them. No sense of individuality remains. Gone is any sense of character or Soul.

"Wheresoever you go, go with all your heart."

Confucius

In the following pages, "prescriptions" are periodically sug-gested, many of which include writing prompts. Why the word "prescription?"

The majority of my clients find being given "homework" in between sessions has given them stepping stones that work to build the best life they are seeking. Those who have not are like patients who have not taken a prescribed pill. Prescribed courses of action do not work if action has not been taken, much like an antibiotic that stays in the bottle instead of being swallowed.

Most people are afraid that their private writing may be read by intruding eyes. To handle that, I have two suggestions: get a separate private journal for the writing exercises that you keep in a secure place. Or if you write in this book, do this in your own private code. (I have written so much in books that I have instructed my daughter to check books before giving them away!)

CHAPTER 1

Preparing the Foundation

In Jungian training, I was told that our deepest roots are located in our greatest hell. Freely translated, this means that all of what we have denied ourselves about our True Self; all that we have unconsciously censored and covered up in order to be seen, heard, and accepted still exists in our unconscious. Think of this treasure as forgotten, relegated to neglected, dusty boxes stored in the darkest corner of our Being basement.

As a means of giving meat to the bones of building a better heart-led life, I have incorporated true stories from real life, both my own and those of a few clients (identities changed) to make the corner-stone principles concrete.

Just Passing Through

For quite some time, since completing my last book, *Nightlight: Soul Calling, Body Listening, Heart Speaking*, I have received many messages from readers asking me to address the topic before you. Their themed request is to lay out what it means to really build a better life. A really good question, don't you think?

Their request is something I've been pondering nearly every day. Today, as I was heading home after my walk, I came across three Hispanic men taking their lunch break in seriously hot weather, betrayed by sweat-soaked orange neck scarves. Suddenly, it dawned on me that these guys might be able to help solve a really rich puzzle.

I decided to 'go for it,' as those who know me know is my nature. Stopping on the curb, I expressed my ignorance and asked, "Can you help me? What are the challenges in tearing down old structures and leveling the earth?"

The three looked at one another and grinned. One replied, "Well, the tearing down can be touchy or easy. It all depends on the materials used for the house. The cheapest are easy, as they fall apart. But the sturdy ones, made of really good materials, are another story.

"As for clearing the land, you've got to be really careful. (Juan points down at the pile of dirt. The others nod in agreement.) First, you've got to start digging in the right place. Sometimes, you find electrical wires or gas lines where they shouldn't be. They're dangerous. If you cut in the wrong place, big trouble. But there's a story about a guy that found something amazing under an old house. I don't know if it's true or not. But here's the story:

> A guy found a diamond pendant. So, he takes it to the jewelers to see if it was real, not that fake stuff. It was a real diamond: one karat. Lucky him. I've found diapers, pools of water, and other junk. No diamonds to date. For sure, if I ever found one, I wouldn't be digging dirt! (The men enjoy a good chuckle.) I don't even do lotteries 'cause I'm not lucky.

Juan's story jump-started me to consider our lives. You and I come, pass through, and die. Just like the buildings being leveled, you and I know that our physical body eventually wears out, be it through aging (if we are lucky) or irreparable injury. Our heads know we are on this Earth for a limited stay. Since we don't know, for sure, when our expiration tag will be pulled from the shelf, how are we living before that happens? This very day could be our last. That's a fact.

Yet, it's another thing to digest, accept, and get the message. How are we living today if it were our last? What are we looking for? Diamonds or dirty diapers? Do we believe we have worth that we've not yet discovered, much less dug deep enough to excavate? Do we sense there is more to life? Have you ever felt a vague uncontrollable longing, but haven't been able to identify what, exactly, you are longing for? This is difficult to answer because this invisible something comes from our very life force. But whatever life we have built, deliberately or not, there were stages to what you know as your life today, and another more current and actual fit to what brings you happiness.

Now, when I pick up a book or listen to an Audible, I want to know what the content is about before investing more precious time into it. In other words, I want a 'good return' on my investment! Perhaps this is true for you? What the rest of this book addresses is how to build our best life by digging up the soil and laying the foundation and frame, and completing the construction of a more natural expression of who we are, bottom line, given the state of this crazy world. How can we come home to ourselves in the most meaningful, loving, and connected way? How can we invite who we really are into public without doing harm to self or others?

We have our old identities. First, we grow up with expectations from parents, schools, communities, and culture. Next, from the particular jobs we did. We might use different costumes as identities. What were yours growing up? For example: as a teen, after school, I served as a 'candy striper' at a local hospital, worked in a department store, and typed the inventories for my father's business in the summers. After college, I served in an Army nursing program. After the Army, I taught and led huge transformational seminars, later practicing as a Jungian psychoanalyst, helping folks decode the guidance their deeper Self was advising through dreams, symptoms, and unexpected experiences. Throughout my saga, I secretly made art, sang, danced, and wrote. Each of these changes was associated with a particular costume, i.e., identity. Each required a different mindset.

As we get older, all of those roles get too tight, not unlike old leather shoes that pinch and blister. We long for something refreshing, and intuit we need a reset. We need a rest. We need to stop striving for more, as well as making ourselves wrong. Like Juan and his crew, we need to dispose of what's on the surface before we can begin the dig home to who we really are. In our life, we know we need to clear out the old closets, drawers, garage, wallet, purse, and/or relationships that leave us drained. Self-doubt and self-criticism have run their course. But the question which remains is where to go from here?

Dear reader, you may have heard it said that "We get what we're looking for." It's easiest not to look. In fact, few people are brave enough to plumb their depths to find their True Self. What is our True Self? Very simply, that which is truest to our nature. No wonder we Jungian analysts refer to the work as "depth psychology." Hence, careful screening is necessary to determine whether the person has the staying power to mine what is hidden, as well as the commitment to stay the course. For this, I look to the unconscious (via dreams, symptoms, meaningful coincidences, etc.) for its consent.

But first, a word about words. The shelves of books or lists of Audibles overflow with words that have no body. Words like the unconscious, ego, diagnosis, and Self. Unfortunately, they are born from a failure of imagination. Why? Simply put, our species responds first to images, having coherence with our heart. Those who risk exploring their interior life must be prepared for hard work. Why? When our Soul wants to be known, said Dr. Carl Jung, She sends out symbols ahead of Herself.

Why is this work so demanding? First, it is the rare person to take on such a journey. That said, I and those whom I work with, experience their mysterious journey as the most important in a lifetime. Second, those who do take on the adventure are rare, indeed, in this

Western world that demands 'fast food' or 'the seven steps' programs purported to bring back our vitality, peace, and ease in the system. The fact is that our most important answers do not come from drive-thru lines, and the 'hurry up, hurry up' mentality of impatience never arrives at our very Soul's guidance.

Just like constructing a strong building, there are stages which proceed reaching who we really were meant to be. We will call each a cornerstone. For what, you might ask? Simply put, to update and honor who you discover you were at the beginning. These cornerstones must be in place to locate infallible guidance; our deepest intuition that never fails. Wisdom is never linear. Wisdom is paradoxical.

Unfortunately, the field of psychology has little to do with accessing joy, wholeheartedness, and freedom to live in ways most natural to our real nature. Mostly, this is because diagnostic terms and theories are inaccessible to the heart. I recall too many lectures and university classes that used bodyless words long grown dusty. How easy to turn the page when words have no tangible substance. How easy to 'space out' or nod off from boredom, or start thinking of things like your to-do list, or a myriad of other thoughts because connecting to what's abstract has no staying power. Unfortunately, the field of psychology has grown as grubby as those dusty theories. The bottom line is that historically psychology overlooks the fact that what we are really looking for is more aliveness.

Thankfully, the Colorado company, Heart Math, has turned our beliefs on their head. According to their impressive research, before we can increase our awareness, there must be an alignment between our head and emotions, aligned with our heart. When this happens, we experience coherence, deepening our infallible intuitive guidance system.

CHAPTER 2

A Vital Discovery

The one thing I know for certain, is this: we are here as an instrument of something immeasurably bigger than our pea brain believes. We are here to contribute something special, even if we are but 'grains of sand.' Even if we've made mistakes. What I do know for sure is that whatever your hidden offering, it's unique. Just like snowflakes. The truth is, if you and I want to build our best heart-led life, we've got to be willing to do the dig, get muddy, and even sweat when the going gets tough.

Over the past five decades, I have been invited to places around the globe to assist those wanting to build better lives. Each of us has been in search of that vague 'something more.' Here's the ringer: something more turns out to be something less! Our journey home to discover the metaphorical diamond, hidden within our Natural Self, has been buried beneath false choices, the desire to please, and most of all, a shit load of fear. The bottom line has been, and continues to be, the fact that we are here as an instrument of that which is not only beautiful but harmonizes with the rest of the natural world. We are here to make a difference, the size of which does not matter. Neither does it matter that most of us are clueless as to what this offering is. By now, for those who think this is airy-fairy, you may as well stop reading. Just know what follows can set you free. No judgment. We each have our own way.

Let me backtrack and put it this way: we go along and live our ordinary lives, but inside, most of us secretly know something's 'off.' Clueless as to just what seems off when the feeling escalates, we feel a restless yearning. But, for what?

What's this unnamed push for something to change? Nameless, it's really the urge for Soul retrieval. It is not that we are unaware of what a better life might be. It's more a matter that we have wandered away from our own center, sometimes called the Middle Path, which leads, infallibly, to your deepest Wisdom.

No need to blame ourselves. Given the constant barrage of social media promises for shortcuts, sooner or later we discover they are a bunch of baloney. Our restlessness resumes. The truth is we've become people who look outside ourselves for answers. (Check out any mall, where the many hunt for the more, which will not satisfy their inner hunger.) We follow others' recipes for Soul nourishment to no avail.

Thousands of clients and university students (male and female) have told me that they were taught to please. But 'being nice,' or 'putting on a happy face,' or gathering the symbols of success is dangerous. Like when roofs or siding begin deteriorating, something must be done to renew our aliveness. Otherwise, the dryness, boredom, and numbness belies a buried Wild One within, begging for attention.

You might be wondering what I mean by the name "Wild One." The name actually came from a client I've known for some time. After summer vacation, he came for a session. He said, "Thank heaven I am back with my Wild Mother!"

Huh? He went on to explain. "When I was growing up, there were so many things I wasn't allowed to express or be, endless rules from home and school. I was a good little lad, so I fell into line. Later, it was the same thing at work. Until I didn't know who I was anymore. But here, I am encouraged to let all that go to discover who I really am."

To my ears, the Wild One or Wild Mother is attuned to all creation, including who we are at our core. But over time, all the aforementioned become stumbling blocks.

Like those hidden gas lines and electrical wires Juan described at that construction site, our original nature, our Wild Nature, exists within but must be sought. Here's a mental image of Wild One: just think of a cat bearing its claws when unhappy, or gently purring when an overdue petting commences. Does the cat need to be taught her responses? No way, Jose. Simply put, the feline is being aligned with its nature, as opposed to being taught.

No product, shortcut, webinar, or guru can give us our answer. No matter how much we pay with money, we remain bored and boring, pale, listless, weak, disappointed one more time.

The attempt to buy ourselves out of unhappiness or sheer boredom does not work because it hides our original nature, which does not buy into politics and political correctness. (Some prefer to name our Wild One within as the portal to intuition.) Either way, whatever you call it, the fact is that you and I house it at our very core. To discover it, I'm bound to tell you that we must resign ourselves to give up the hunt to "be somebody" or to "get somewhere." Whatever holds us to the same old, same old must go. This is scary business.

CHAPTER 3

What Must We Do?

What makes letting go of what's not working so darn hard? What helps us turn away from empty promises? Pure and simply put we are comfort-seeking creatures, as is any cat worth her salt, seeking sunny spots to chill. Our inner predator, fear, will convince us to stay comfy. While clearing the decks, so to speak, of past comfort sources in the outer world may sound good, the fact is that to "Marie Kondo" (let go of whatever doesn't spark your joy) our life can pull us into extreme vulnerability. Who wants to be exposed? Heart-led living requires giving up all distractions, visiting the inexplicable, yet finding deeper footing on planet Earth. For this, we need to dig deeper to discover the discarded parts of ourselves that take us not to 'dirty diapers' thinking, but toward the treasure that we house. Yep, right around the corner comes fear predator.

So, what can we do to avoid as much manipulation from fear? First, buckle up, buttercup. Fasten your seat belt. The following may well be uncomfortable. It does, however, work. Overall, each of the following steps assists our heart to have more courage and makes our ego (who we might call 'King Know-It-All') step aside. Let me add that while the ego, our belief about who we must be, is important to function in this world (without which we end up in the loony bin), its need for the throne drowns out the whisper of heart guidance, which, Heart Math has found to be 5,000 times more powerful than the head. That said, here we go for those who want Cliff's Notes and don't want to read further:

1. Clear space. Ditch all excesses.

2. Suffer no fools.

3. Know that setbacks are not mistakes. They are part of the creative process.

4. Tend your creative fire, even if this means allowing yourself five minutes in the beginning to do absolutely nothing.

5. Toss out to-do lists.

6. Sort out the people who support your dig and walk away from the rest.

7. Ditch the naysayers, including toxic family members and seasonal friends.

8. Don't expect applause.

9. Clear the ground for the unnatural and inexplicable.

10. Delete anything that depletes your energy.

11. Sacrifice the artificial.

12. Pay attention to dreams. Here's a common example: the dreamer is blocked from movement; maybe the car, truck, bus, or whatever, refuses to move. That part of his/her underground is asking the dreamer to shift the attitude he/she is maintaining that reveals a stuck attitude.

Truthfully, these twelve tasks sound much easier to accomplish than it might seem.

At the end of our life here on Earth, we are asked two questions:

1. How did you love?

2. How did you serve?

How do I know? Fifty years ago, I did a residency with Elisabeth Kubler Ross, the Swiss physician who brought/started hospice in America and explored dying and the afterlife. What she found is NOT theory. Rather, we interviewed some folks who had been clinically dead. Not all of them saw 'the light,' as is so often reported. However, our interviewees were consistent in being asked the above questions. You might say they are our final pop quiz from the Great Beyond. Those questions have guided my life ever since.

Be assured you are more courageous than most. Simply because you dare to be here, keeping me company. Not everyone is brave enough, you know. Take the next few minutes to imagine you were called here to creatively express a message. Imagine that your message, your life, were some form of a love letter or project reflecting your heart's deepest desire which serves others, and that which is beyond human understanding. This, my friend, is the Truth.

Likewise, the following will support your journey:

Spend time in silence and nature.

Each day, ask yourself: for what are you grateful?

Drop all performances. For example: let go of the need to be too sweet. Trying too hard to please distracts from what's sacred.

Close loops: bring to closure what is important to your heart that has not known completion.

CHAPTER 4

Beginning the
Dig to Mother Earth

We think we know who we are. I understand. For much of my life, I thought I knew who I was, too. Simple, right? We know our birthdate, name, and so on. But one day, walking along the shores of Lake Washington, the thought came to me that maybe we could look at our lives here on planet Earth as analogous to seeing it as a chance to live as if we were a human love letter. What are we writing with our lives today? This past week?

We have our old identities. First, we grow up with expectations from parents, schools, communities, and our culture. Next, from the particular jobs we hold. We might think of these identities as different costumes. What were yours growing up? (For example: as a teen, after school I served as a 'candy striper' at a local hospital, worked in a department store, and typed the inventories for my father's business in the summers. After college, I served in an Army nursing program, and later, I taught, led huge transformational seminars, eventually practicing as a Jungian psychoanalyst, helping folks decode the guidance their deeper Self was advising (dreams, symptoms, unexpected experiences). Throughout my saga, I secretly made art, sang, danced, and wrote. Each of these changes were associated with a particular costume (i.e., identity). Each required a different mindset.

Later, I realized that I am a project person. I could not do the same thing forever, like those who stay in the same job for fifty years. As my Southern friend would say, "Bless their little sweet heart." The way I've lived has never been an assembly line approach. I thought I knew who I was via professional identities and university degrees: nurse practitioner, clinical psychologist, Jungian analyst. Over time, I discovered those roles were not the Mother Lode.

As we get older, all of those roles get too tight, not unlike old leather shoes that pinch and blister. We long for something refreshing and intuit we need a reset. We need a rest. We need to stop striving for more, as well as making ourselves wrong. Like Juan and his crew, we need to dispose of what's on the surface before we can begin the dig home to who we really are. In our life, we know we need to clear out the old (closets, drawers, garage, wallet, purse, and/or relationships that leave us drained). Self-doubt and self-criticism have run their course. But the question which remains is 'where to from here?'

In 2012, while ambivalent about 'where to go next,' I found myself in that peculiar situation known as 'the Field of Opposites.' When you are confronting polar opposites, the important thing to keep in mind is that tension always precedes new growth. A current example in America is the great divide between MAGA people who support Trump, and those across the aisle who are more than fearful that if he gets reelected, it will be the end of American democracy. The same tension is present between those who want to ban abortion and those who don't; as well as those who are concerned about global warming and those who deny it is happening.

Major events of this world, and our unrehearsed responses to them, just might give us a clue as to where to begin our own dig. On December 14, 2012, the news left the world horrified. On that fateful day in Newtown, Connecticut, at Sandy Hook Elementary School, twenty children aged six to seven, along with six adults, were killed by a teenaged boy armed with a gun. (Yes, he most likely had a Sensory Deficit Disorder, and most likely was on the Asperger's Spectrum, with a history, since age two, of disabilities. Yet these probable conditions do not explain his killing spree. Many suffer, but they do not replicate what the killer felt compelled to carry out.) Since that day, the number of mass murders in America has tripled.

Please note, this book is not about murder or mayhem. (We have enough of that in the evening news.) But it was that particular event that initiated my Soul search into the purpose of being on this Earth during these times. Discovering it changed my life and deepened my faith in the Beyond, freeing myself from time wasters.

From the Sandy Hook massacre, I was reminded of the impact on the dead children's siblings. Let me explain. On March 21st, 1991 my only son died violently in a car accident with a drunk driver. He left behind his eight-year-old sister, who adored everything about her "Mattie." Too often the trauma to siblings of loss is overlooked, especially the little ones, who developmentally grieve in hidden ways when compared to adults. With this memory in mind, after the Sandy Hook massacre, my attention went not only to the parents (I knew that one), but to the sisters and brothers of the murdered. But, and this was a big 'but,' what could I do?

Clueless, I did what I always do, I meditated. What I did not expect was the imagery that came. There was the image of the world, and a woman who looked like Mary atop it. Roses were all around her. Then two spotlights appeared: one on Peru, the other on Connecticut. Just then, the woman held up a bundle, let it unfurl down over the planet, and it turned out to be a quilt.

As an aside, but a vital one, I was not a stranger to the importance that a handmade quilt could bring to the recipient. I remembered the most important gift I'd ever been given: Carrie's quilt. Here's the story: my mother told me that my spiritually-adopted grandmother was concerned as to what she could give me for my twenty-first birthday. For my sister Linda's twenty-first birthday the year before, she had given Linda a pin (the pins photo may be seen in my third book called *Nightlight: My Soul Calling, Body Listening, Hear Soeaking*). Not just any pin: this gold-encrusted pin was one that Carrie's grandfather gave her that he had been given from the plantation owner when slaves were freed. The story goes that the owner was fearful of what might happen when he and his family headed north. So, he told Carrie's grandpa to use it as a trade for a bag of potatoes if they began to starve.

Back to my upcoming twenty-first birthday. What to do? Since Carrie had given her most valuable possession, the pin, she had nothing left to give me. Carrie found her answer through prayer. At eighty-six years old and nearly blind, Carrie spent evening after evening stitching together with red thread small pieces of fabric that came from significant memories: her wedding dress, her twenty-fifth anniversary dress from when she celebrated with her now long-departed husband Archie, her mother's dress, and even patches from the baby clothes of her sons who died in early childhood. When my birthday came, she said the following: "Now listen, child. When I made this, I sang a song or did a prayer with each stitch. This is to be a 'panic blanket' for you and for your babies and grandbabies. Always remember my love is with you." Carrie died six weeks later.

Now, with the horrible news of the mass killing at Sandy Hook Elementary, that memory came back in full force. I went through the gamut with the vision I was given. What was creative imagination's imagery trying to tell me? In laser-like speed, I had my answer. I put out a 'call to action' on social media for those who would be willing to do something similar to what Carrie had done for me for the Sandy Hook siblings. I called it the Love Project. That call brought a number of mothers, grandmothers, daughters, and other females who created lap-sized quilts for those children who had lost their brothers or sisters. The rule was that while working on it, there could be no internet, television, or any noise at all so they could fill their quilt with song and prayer.

Throughout the process, unaware of the next step, the Predator (fear) stepped in, with its strong, intimating whisper: What if this doesn't work? (It did.) What is the basis of decision making as to which child should receive which quilt anonymously? (I was given a list of each child's name, and the quilters themselves chose.) What if you don't get all the quilts?

Just after the third quilt arrived, the Predator tried to dampen hope with whispers: 'What if the rest don't come?' (All arrived in time.) How will you get them there the day before the first anniversary? (A sister of a colleague asked her sister, a flight attendant for Delta Airlines, to comp the flight. They did.) What if there are too many obstacles? (They came up at every step.) Who would photograph the creations for free? (A neighbor of one of the quilters showed up, unasked, and offered to comp the pictures. She was a professional photographer.) Where would I deliver them? (Finally, I found the name of a church near the school.) The day my husband and I arrived with the quilts, near the school, we found Saint Rose of Lima. Aha! The reference in the meditation imagery uniting Peru with Connecticut came together. What a relief.

The lessons the entire process brought home to me were:

1. Ambivalence is the first cousin to inspiration.
2. Mistrust of that invisible something, stops myriad acts of kindness.
3. There is an innate goodness in strangers who dare to give in a way that defies logic.

Those with open-heartedness show up for duty, even though they do not know how to proceed. They say 'yes' to the unknown and

Unknowable. Their hearts guide them toward nurturing, not their egos' fear of failure. (For more on this and photos, see carabarker.com and *Nightlight: My Soul Calling, Body Listening, Heart Speaking.*) What I can tell you with certainty is that the whole Love Project was a concrete demonstration that an acorn (say inspiration) can become a mighty oak under the right conditions. (Which, by the way, begins with the cold. Anyone who has experienced deep grief is aware of those waves of cold that come and go.)

To be completely transparent, I should tell you that half of the women had never quilted before. A third had never threaded a needle since home economics class in middle school. And yet, something more powerful than discomfort ignited a spark in their hearts to go forward with a concrete attempt to help affirm the world is caring as well as cruel. What a relief for us each to have something to create from our heart's longing that words cannot touch in response to the unspeakable.

No matter how we might like to stop the future, life keeps rolling along and bringing unexpected challenges to our door, all of which force us to reconsider what we really know about ourselves. If the challenges are big enough, doing the dig to who we really are is helpful.

A Building Metaphor

As a little girl, I'd heard something that may be familiar to you: "Build your house upon a rock. If yours is on sand, the wind and rain will take it out." Makes sense, doesn't it? Rocks are strong. Loose sand is not. An incorrect relationship with what scares the Dickens out of us, dear reader, is as loose sand, far from the bedrock which will later support construction of a firm foundation. This can only be found with willingness to do a dig down to our roots.

One of the times this is helpful is when we become parents. We want our children to be happy. Heck, we want to be happy ourselves.

But, by the time we are this age, we know that some of our choices have been better than others. We want to save our kids from the mistakes we made. (Usually, we can't.) We want to prepare the atmosphere so that more of life's good can come through the door.

And, yet, if we are completely honest, we know that we cannot protect our young from psychologically burning their fingers on the stove, as well as frustration, disappointments, hurt feelings, being misunderstood, these days, fears of school shootings, and sometimes, the unseen. We cannot protect them from the darker side of life, where fear 'hangs out,' no matter their present age. Unfortunately, darkness is the compost for growth. Decay precedes beauty. All we can do is search to discover our own Way through the good, the bad, the ugly, and that old bug-a-boo Predator that we call fear.

The question today, and all the tomorrows is where does your heart want you to go? We cannot parent well unless we know how to parent ourselves best. I remember when my teenage daughter said to me, "Mom, if you don't go to Zurich for your training, how am I supposed to 'go for it' when I am your age?" Busted. Our kids have an amazing way of mirroring back to us ourselves. At the time, I was mentally trying to figure out the pros and cons of such a decision. Brandy reminded me of the infallible guidance that lives below the neck. She was right.

So, the issue is not what does your head think you should do, but rather how can you dig down to your deepest level of knowing your heart and Soul. Your answer depends on who you think you are and what invisible fear blocks you. If you believe you are here to just 'get through the day,' well, there's not much I can say to help. (If this is you, please put the book down and give it away.) If, on the other hand, you believe that like every single life form in nature, like the acorn, you, too, are here to evolve with the purpose to bloom, well, alrighty then, we can begin. Everything in the natural world (of which we are a part) is hard-wired to grow, to bloom. We must, however, be willing to take life as it comes. That, in itself, is a pretty big deal when it comes to wake-up calls. Even they do not come in linear ways but unfurl like the fern in the forest.

Life is a labyrinth. We have dreams, hopes, losses, and down-ward-slides. How kind will life be to our kids? Our grandkids? How kind has it been to you? We have infinite choices to quit, to roll over, to sit on the sidelines, to play dead. Or we can get out there on the field. We can set out to discover the secret to getting more out of life, embracing today's chance to live freely and wholeheartedly as a vehicle of love. Here's what I want to ask you, for real, for real: Why wait?

You have the right, you know, like everyone else, to throw off the shackles of a life grown flat. Consider what Juan and crew were doing after the old structure was torn down. To create something new, the old and worn out had to go before the dig. Regardless our challenge, like all living things, you and I are here to grow and to transform our losses into something beautiful, bold, meaningful, and wise. (Think, folks, like Michael J. Fox, who uses his catalyst of Parkinson's Disease to bring awareness and research for others.) We are talking about your own freedom! Your own song to sing.

CHAPTER 5

What Helps Us Be Best Prepared for Our Dig?

You have your own history and examples. But in my house, I remember no one sat down with me and told me how to grow forward when my baby sister died. Likewise, when I had to tell my daughter that her brother, her hero, had died when she was only eight, there was no instruction manual, no way to barricade her from the pain, and, just as important, no secret book which could guarantee that she could get more out of life through navigating the worst of the worst, even this. No, her veil of innocence had been pierced with the shock, and she is not alone. We all have our own stories of severed innocence, which forced us to let go of what we valued. In its absence, the dig begins.

For most of us, we bumble through the unexpected without being told just how we might do our best. If there is a book of secrets, it has eluded us. More a matter of 'figure it out on your own,' as one young man who came from a family of abuse and addiction recently told me. In my case, I began to notice something crucial that sent me on a quest for the answer. What is the secret to building our best life and releasing the fears that stop us, regardless of what happens?

For years, I've observed something puzzling. You probably have, too. How is it that equally lousy things can happen to a number of people, and have completely different outcomes? Why do some fold up their tents and give up on life, whereas others find a way to thrive? Yes, yes, resilience is a strong key. But I did not know that then. And, even if I had, I still noticed that even when good things happen, some cannot seem to take in the good, instead calling in more drama; whereas others seem to call in a never-ending stream of events, experiences, and conditions which fan the flames of gratitude. So, what's the secret?

Let's dig deeper. There is a true story that my friend and colleague, Greg Furth, told me about a pair of twins. One had become a remarkably successful surgeon. The other was homeless and an alcoholic. Individually, each was asked, "How do you account for the way your life has turned out?" Each answered the same way: "My father."

Those who know the secret to living a wholehearted life have a different answer to the question 'just who do you think you are,' than those who don't. Why? What is their secret Way through life so they come up with the 'more' we seek if we accepted full freedom? Somehow, they have done a deeper exploration of their inner landscape. What this provides is a more expansive perspective. It all comes down to how we are accustomed to framing our situation. (For more on this see Section 3: Framing.)

As you turn each page, it is my wish that you make one fundamental decision, which is this: decide to have a heart for yourself as you discover its longing bit by bit. Commit to keeping your 'eye on the prize.' Hang on. Open to the possibility that we are not alone. Together we will uncover the other three secret cornerstones, beginning with what is needed to build your strongest foundation to support your personal freedom; to let you live a life guided by your heart. I know this for a fact: doing what follows will yield far less strain on your system. For as John Eldridge says so wisely: "... when we lose the heart's longing, its secret life, we are lost."

Shifting life from lost to found comes when we reclaim this longing, for this is our own unique Way composed from the four cornerstones, anchoring the foundation for a more solid, creative, and living a life that is true to who you are that's been hiding. Consider beginning with your own story.

Love Abounds Original painting (in color) by Cara Barker, 1991

How much room have you left for the possibility that you are not alone? How willing have you been up to now to leave more room for the Mystery that lives beyond the intellect? **You do not have to park your brain at the door to do so.**

CHAPTER 6

Someone's Altered my Blueprint

One thing's for certain. You, like the rest of us, sincerely want to live the best life you can. Isn't this true? You want your legacy to demonstrate greater aliveness, vitality, joy, connection, and abundance. You want to be at home with yourself, no matter where you are, without either pretense or mask. So did I for years before I discovered how to get through all that striving that got in my way of living and loving freely.

When you do not bring forward what is within you, what is within you will destroy you. But when you bring forth what is within you, what is within you will heal and save you.

Gnostic Gospel of Saint Thomas

Nothing has ever been created that does not share this urge to flourish, progress, and be all that it can be. Nature conspires to endow us with this urge for growth. When nature is blocked, like say, in a log-jam, courtesy of the otters, the water grows stagnant and problems ensue. It's in our very make-up to take developmental leaps: from stories of restriction to new chapters of liberation. Let's say you decide you'd like to make this shift. You suspect there's more joy, aliveness, health, and prosperity you could be enjoying, and you'd also like to spend less time in suffering. You recognize that hanging onto pain no longer serves you. I did. The fact is that I did not know how to advance in that direction.

To move forward, I had to do a deep dig into what story I was living out and figure out what untrue stories I was telling myself. I did not realize I was doing that for many years. We are experiential learners, after all.

When people come to me for advice on how to live their best life, it's helpful to approach their situation as if it were from a story. Of course, to 'pull this off' you've got to take a giant step back from the day-to-day tedium and imagine that like any good theatre, film, or piece of literature, there is an author. You are that author. Maybe you like your narrative so far, maybe you aren't so thrilled with particular sections and could do with a bit of rewrite. If you look at your life as an unfolding tale you are constructing, then it makes it easier to tweak it when it's time for new settings, characters, costumes, and lighting. There are times when your story gets boring, lifeless, and uninspiring, and that's how you know it's time to shift your 'storyline.' Or, as internet sensation Marie Kondo puts it: get rid of everything that doesn't spark joy. Although she is addressing cleaning one's house, the same thing applies to cleaning up our act, making room for more of the new to walk through the door, and sweeping away more of the old and dusty out into the dumpster. This desire is not new. It is the very one your ancestors who walk behind you wished and wanted for you.

One young man came to me last year feeling lost, confused, and blocked. I asked him to "Show me the block." That was his home-work. One week later, he placed his homework before me. Let's call this client Jamie. What he came back with blew me away. With his 3-D printer, Jamie created an ancient stairway. Around three or four steps up, Jamie had placed a clear acrylic barrier. He said, "I feel what blocks me, but can't see it. Whatever it is, it's old and really powerful."

Jamie was absolutely right. The block he experienced was incredibly old, generational, palpable, and stopping him.

Way back to the time when our ancestors sat around the first fire outside the cave, stories were told. We human beings have a love of explanation, solving problems, and crafting dreams come true. We love to propose not only explanations, but what really turns us on, at least for those whose attitudes haven't rigidified and turned hopelessly stale and spiritually arthritic, is possibilities. Wouldn't you love more freedom? More inspiration and delight? Only the walking dead have given up this desire. They are what I call 'the grey people,' not to make them wrong, but those who prefer the role of victim can only cast blame. (For a rich source of blame, have a peek at politicians trying to justify their lack of cooperation.)

The Question

So, how do we shift from the stale to the fresh? How do you snap out of feeling lousy to feeling good? How do we move from the ho-hum to the magnificent? What's the key? What's the secret that Wisdom Teachers have known for ages that escapes us while we are manic in our obsession with technological gadgets? The Masters know that the only way to get through a logjam is to shift from head-centered to heart-centered living. Why wait until it's too late? Why is this so vital?

Our thoughts create our reality. Science has proven this to be true through neurobiologists and neuroscientists. With the decline of institutions, governments, economic, and biophysical thriving around the globe, there is an increasing conversation about the need for us to awaken as a human race. What this means is that humankind cannot evolve until we expand the story of who we are and come into a fuller, more meaningful relationship with our True Nature. Little children are the best example: hopping around, dancing where no one else is dancing, giggling up a storm. We forget that we, too, have the right to act with wild abandon. But first, you and I have to 'get over ourselves' and give up the injunctions against being truly natural. This requires expanding our true relationship with the Universe. Without retrieving your focus in this way, nothing will change. Without this courageous act, this leap of faith into a deeper relationship with the Spirit of who you are, life remains a mechanical repetition, an endless *Groundhog Day*-like loop. Until our self-concept expands, we settle. Please note that by expanding our lives, I do NOT mean adding more layers or more acts, but quite the opposite. Think of the opposite as cleaning out the closet of what no longer works or delights you. Predicting the future with such a clearing is none of our business, and doesn't work anyway, does it?

It is no wonder that the greatest stories revolve around the lives of those who have made the shift from head to heart. Without this, we simply cannot come home to who we really are. Let's look at just a few famous examples: How about Saint Francis? The son of one of the five wealthiest families in Assisi, the stage had been set for

Francis to take over the highly prosperous business his father had built. Before he went off with his buddies to join the Crusades, there was no indication whatsoever that Francis wished for anything more than what his father wanted for him: building more wealth. But, like every heroic tale, Francis met the enemy, and as Pogo put it, the enemy was within. Francis came face to face with the consequences of living a story which was based on outer wealth.

Do few things, but do them well.

Saint Francis

He did not know that his heart was un-awakened. He did not know he was sleepwalking and blocked, like the masses, until he bottomed out in a life-threatening illness and coma. Before his near-death, he had not discovered the secrets behind living the life he wanted. He did not know how to identify what he wanted until his life began to unravel. It was only after this close encounter with death, and the dying to his old life, that Francis came back to life.

Another Illustration

Hundreds of years later, in the twentieth century Nazi concentration camps, Viktor Frankl's story came to an end quite literally. For many years, Frankl devoted himself, among other things, to writing his opus: a manuscript that contained all he held most sacred. If you've ever heard him speak, or read his magnificent *Man's Search for Meaning*, you know that just as he was stripped of his material possessions at that death camp, his manuscript was burned. Devastated, he watched his life work go up in flames. Later, the ovens killed those he loved. Frankl, like Francis, turned to his heart and aligned with what he found there: the secrets to his own life meaning. This was, however, not before he allowed himself to "die" to his old life. He was not alone. I, too, have had to metaphorically die many times, casting aside worn out identities and letting them, too, go up in flames.

Meanwhile, in another camp, Elie Wiesel and his family were having another Holocaust experience. Described in *Night*, he reconstructs how he not only endured Auschwitz, but how he shifted his life story. But, to get there, like Saint Francis and Frankl, he had to dig deeper into the ground of his essential being. Today, he is a Nobel Peace Prize Laureate. Anything is possible if we are willing to make a shift from how we have lived up until this point to a more expansive and deeply moving story aligned with who we truly are. Without discovering this secret, feeling good will never last long, for we are not yet free.

Anything is possible if you are willing to live a deeply authentic life!

Cara Barker

We Are Both the Prison Guard and Prisoner

It's no small wonder that any story of merit involves the hero's struggle to either pass by the dragon or get swallowed. Let's see how this might play out across the sea. Emmet Fox tells a story from the Middle Ages. The legend is that a man is captured by the baron's soldiers and thrown into an underground dingy dungeon. Now and then, the guards threw some bread and a bit of water between the bars. Twenty years went by like this. One day, the man, grown weary, in desperation, decided that death is preferable to this lowly existence, and threw himself against the prison bars, expecting a strong reaction from the guards and sudden death, which would have ended his misery. Instead, the prison door opened! No one bothered to stop him from climbing the stairs or crossing through the courtyard. He went home. This man spent two decades of his life in a cell that was never locked, except in his own mind. What about you?

This archetypal story is as true today as when it was first told. Forty-nine years ago, my own son, Matt, around three years old at the time, began howling from the bathroom for me to let him out. "It's locked, Mama," he cried, pounding on the door.

"Turn the handle, Matti," I said. "Just turn the handle."

"I can't. It won't open."

More pounding. More tears. A few moments later, a crack of light appeared beneath the door, and two sheepish coal black eyes peeped out. "It was locked on the inside, Mama."

Which Story Are You Living?

Make no mistake about it. Opening our self-imposed, unconscious doors to our freedom does not happen overnight. Becoming visible is a real struggle. We carry on our backs these invisible but heavy burlap bags stuffed with our own self-imposed limiting stories. Just because we might be skilled at something does not mean we are locked into that role. We commit to self-limiting beliefs impeding our dig down to the truth of who we are as though they were the Gospel. When I was much younger, I was lucky enough to witness the great Buddhist teacher, Thich Nhat Hanh, tell a story from across the sea. As I recall, a peasant man came home one day to discover that his hut was completely aflame. Desperately searching for his tiny boy, all he could find was ashes. Time went by, as the man grieved for his lost son. Many years later, there was a knock on the door of the reconstructed hut. "Father," said the voice of a young man, "let me in. I've come home."

"Leave me alone," protested the father. "My son is dead, and you are cruel. Leave me alone."

After several more pleas from the young man, the father remained devoted to his grieving and did not budge. The son, who had escaped the fire, went away, never to return. He had come home but was not welcomed.

Some twelve years after I heard this story, it came back to haunt me when my own son was killed. Was I to become like the grieving father who denied himself the gift of life?

True, my son would not return, at least not in the same physical form. I decided then and there to metaphorically keep the door to my heart unlocked. I can tell you this: I've had many, many experiences of my boy through the experience of witnessing other children and college-age kids (which he was when he died) just enjoying life as only kids can. True, in the beginning, these moments were bittersweet. But, over the years, I wouldn't trade them for anything. I know my son would want me to "stay in the game," just as your family members would wish for you.

Our Stories Shift as We Shift

For instance, I could not have imagined myself having paranormal experiences with Matt after his death, much less sharing them. (You will find them described in my last book entitled *Nightlight: My Soul Calling, Body Listening, Heart Speaking*.)

But even that is part of my story, just as you have the unexpected peppering your own. Maybe not with the supernatural, but in some fashion, something has spoken to your heart. We do not know why we've got the particular details in our stories the way we do. All I know is that whatever comes into your life is there with purpose; there to expand your way of retrieving your focus, there to help you and me grow. We are here so you and I can take up the life that's truly ours to live out in a fresher, more life-giving way than ever before. I love how author Madeleine L'Engle put it when I took my daughter to New York when she was a little girl to meet her favorite writer. Madeleine told her, "Always follow what your heart tells you. If you do, you will never go wrong. When you grow up, choose something to do that makes you happy."

How Has Your Script Changed?

Not a day goes by in my consulting room when I do not hear this sentiment. Some come to me having suffered reverses in terms of health, wealth, love life, career, or the process of aging. Some of you are smack dab in the middle of the throes of grief. Some of you find yourselves inexplicably growing bored with what used to satisfy. Some have lost your passion.

Some have never found it. Only this morning, I sat with a man who has devoted his whole life to banking, only to discover, in a failing economy, that he feels bankrupt inside.

When his father wanted him to be a banker, he gave up his own passion for flying, for becoming a pilot. That was fifty years ago. Today, all the bells and whistles of outer success are leaving him flat. During his deep dig into his Truth, he realized his lines were changing. How about you? What's changing in your life? If you are willing to be completely truthful to yourself, what might you admit is shifting?

Take a moment to answer these questions:

What's shifting in my life story is:

_____

_____

_____

What I want to shift in my story is:

_____

_____

_____

_____

What I want more of is:

_____

_____

_____

_____

CHAPTER 7

A Time for Telling Ourselves the Truth

What do you do during shifting times in your life like this? Look to what you need. Consider the following three essential questions:

1. What's lacking in your life story?

2. Where's the excess in your life that's suffocating your Spirit and crowding out new life? What's in the way of your digging deeper to know? Another way of putting this goes back to Juan and those unexpected gas lines and electrical wires obstructing their dig.

3. Are you willing to take a leap of faith?

I'm reminded of an amazing woman we'll call Lenore, who came to me with these concerns long ago. Trained as an engineer, she found herself feeling depleted much of the time, and so she joined one of the groups I run which uses painting as a means of engaged meditation. This courageous woman took her process seriously and followed her heart's nudging to delve into expressive arts. She was completely unaware of this desire at the beginning of her process. As she learned to trust herself more, something greater than her previously limited self-concept began to guide her forward. Using her love of color, form, and connection as a cornerstone to realign her focus, her life, and her offering, she went on to become an art therapist (a career that did not even exist when she went to the university as a young adult). Today, she's thriving. No guts, no glory.

Sometimes, we've just got to let go of the old props to discover new, unexplored rooms in our hearts. But first, the deep dig. This is not to say there's no price tag. There is. If your life stays small, you pay. If you follow your heart's nudging, you pay. Either way, we pay. Sometimes, we've just got to accept the old way isn't working before things get better. To arrive at this place, we have to let go of everything in the way of our dig down to what's deepest in us crying out for attention.

Improving our situation depends upon our willingness to realign our focus, gradually releasing old props. Many years ago, some medicine people I knew called this "Soul Retrieval." Here, we'll refer to it as a "focus retrieval." It's so easy to get lost these days, isn't it? We are drowning like the Sorcerer's Apprentice trying to do what is not for us. We got tricked by our monkey mind's curiosity, putting on airs, trying to be who we aren't. This holds true also for those who try to shrink down, stay unnoticed, and settle for less.

God strips us of our props.

Meister Eckhart

Meanwhile, we neglect our hearts' desire and relegate it to "the bench" for a later time, which never comes. We will never come fully alive by hanging on to our contingency plans and hedging our bets.

The time does come, you know, when the unpicked fruit on the apple tree goes to rot. We can wait too long and miss our chance.

Sorry to say it, but I owe you the truth. I learned this from our apple tree that popped out 400 pounds per year, and too many went to waste. How much applesauce and how many apple pies can you make with that quantity? The answer was to share the pickings. We are, after all, here to share. What a difference this mentality would make in our world.

What Can You Do?

If you don't want to miss your turn, take it. Claim your right to live your nature out loud, out freely. Clear the area for your dig. This means you must retrieve the secret truthful focus of your heart, which is hidden on the surface of your life. And when you reach ground zero, put the treasure you find into circulation that not only benefits you, but those in need.

Now, it is one thing to visualize how the construction worker digs down through concrete and dirt before the building can be constructed. But quite another when we are talking about digging down deep in ourselves.

What does this really mean? And, more importantly, where do you look? I can tell you as a Jungian Analyst, we look to where undiscovered answers live, in the unconscious, where the treasure lies. Along with the client, we explore their dreams as well as body signs and symptoms to uncover the unconscious and infallible guidance to move forward in building a better life.

My research has shown that the World Weary strivers who rush through life at warp speed unfortunately look in the wrong place for solutions. They look to their intellect or to the outer world for what other people think they should do. This tendency never produces truly satisfying answers.

Time for Realignment

Think about it. If your spine is out of whack you get it realigned, maybe see a chiropractor. For a car misalignment, you go to a trusty mechanic's shop and get the correction. Otherwise, you cannot move properly in the world. Without realignment, you cannot function productively. Not unlike this morning when the pain of a muscle cramp near my right shoulder drew all work to a standstill. Before I one step further, I had to do what my mother advised in Finnish, loosely translated as 'tend to your own knitting.' The body does not lie, overriding the head's to-do list. We do well to listen.

What's a Good First Step?

Imagine and recall just what you've been giving your focus to. Let's take this step by step:

STEP 1

Consider the invisible sign, so to speak, you've been carrying around in your head, and adjust it to something more expansive; more empowering. By way of example, just the other day, I saw a homeless man standing by the onramp to the freeway. He'd scrawled the word "Needy" on it. This was the sign he was holding, the prison of his thinking. (I know this might sound unkind, but I am just reporting the facts.) The next day, a young woman in the University District held a placard that said: "Pregnant. Struggling. Need help." This is the sign she holds, reflecting to herself how small she holds herself. She settles. The question is: what invisible sign are you holding?

How do you wish your story might change? Where have you been putting your focus? On the appearance of lack, or on the experience of bounty? Do you have the guts to live out the marvel of your nature, even if you doubt there is anything marvelous in you at all? Are you living out the Truth of who you are at the most essential level or living a lie? The real turning points in life come when we are willing to let go and press up against the bars of our cage (the self-limiting thoughts) and leverage up. But first, the mud. For example, one of my own limiting beliefs is 'I don't have time.' So, when a space opens up, I promise myself to take up what I've been procrastinating doing, such as reviewing Spanish and trying another form of Yoga. When I overcommit, I know it's time to take a break and ask myself which focus informs my heart best?

Prescription

Reflect on the invisible sign you've been schlepping around that isn't bringing you what you want. Write it down. What metaphorical 'sign' would you like to carry that would honor who you are? Hint: this sign would realign you with confidence. Write it out.

Reread it every day, four times a day.* Notice what happens to your new, revised story about who you most wish to become. Stand tall. You are not alone. Repeat your retrieved focus. Relax. You are on your way. Start by filling out the following:

Fill in the "invisible sign" you've been carrying that holds you too small.

The 'me' that settles for too little.

Now, consider the "sign" you'd like to carry invisibly that best reflects how you'd love to expand your self-concept.

The 'me' that feels worthy and deserving of feeling great much more of the time.

* Note: Here's one crucial distinction between those who are most successful in discovering a more enlivening way to life and those who are not. Those who thrive do not skip steps or take shortcuts. (This is not a scolding, simply what I've observed over many years working with people who want to transform their lives.) They write out, reread, and realign every day without exception. This requires letting go of excuses, self -justifications, and the penchant to avoid.

What I didn't realize before about the 'invisible sign' I've been carrying, and what it is attracting into my life is:

I am _____

_____

_____

_____

_____

_____

_____

_____

The benefit of my newly-revised, preferred sign, would be:

_____

_____

_____

For me:

_____

_____

_____

_____

For others:

_____

_____

_____

_____

CHAPTER 8

Digging Down to the Invisible

L et's continue from the last chapter.

STEP 2

Take to heart that you and your evolving story are part of a Bigger Story. Listen to what Princeton researcher Sara Lawrence-Lightfoot quotes from Robert Quinn:

> "There is no longer a feeling of alignment between our inner values and our tasks in the external world. We find ourselves working harder and harder and receiving less satisfaction from our efforts. We struggle through every day lacking the vitality, commitment, and initiative we used to have. After much inner reflection and contemplation, we realize we need a new focus, a new vision, but it's difficult to uncover. How does a person this aimless and dissatisfied find the will to reassert control over life, to rediscover purpose, to tell a story that restores energy, fulfillment, productivity where before there were fatigue, boredom, and despair? By taking control over your story. You must be ready. . . . to rewrite it and rewrite it. . . . what it really is treating your life, this vital and organic thing as a story. . . . Your story has to move you."

As pointed out in the last chapter, our bodies give us invaluable feedback as to when we are, or are not, in alignment. So, you see, we are all in this soup together. We get to choose whether we are going to stick with our old blueprint for how to live a heart-led life (that isn't working) or accept that you and I are far more powerful than we have imagined. Your mind is incredibly powerful; so powerful that the latest findings in neuroscience attest to the fact that what you think about brings about either greater suffering or greater peace. Which do you prefer? Francis, Frankl, and Wiesel did not have this research at their disposal, but they knew intuitively they had choices. They shifted their experience, their relationship with life, their contribution. Your mind is so powerful that it can shift your feelings of deadness to an experience of a greater aliveness. Your thoughts, my friend, produce the type of story you are living and who you are becoming as the main character. All you need remember is the "invisible sign" you've carried thus far in your thinking and replace it with the one you prefer.

So, on the surface of who you've thought you were, what kind of story have you been telling yourself? Consider the past two years. During this period, have you been producing a comedy? A melodrama? A romance? A thriller? A story of lack, or one of liberating abundance? Remember, 'what you think about you bring about.' The real question is: what do you want to bring about from where you are today? Before clearing the land, you and I must address what is no longer needed, and what is, in fact, blocking our way to a heart-led life.

Ask yourself the following, without censorship or edit, and record your truth. If children a hundred years from now were reading about the life you most deeply want to be living, wholeheartedly from this point forward, fill in what you'd like them to read.

(Your first name) (your last name) realized at (present age) years old that what he/she really, most sincerely wanted to create was a life that (describe in detail):

_____

_____

_____

He/she did so by simplifying his/her focus to include spending more time and energy in creating the following experiences:

_____

_____

_____

And wasting less time and energy on:

_____

_____

_____

What created his/her joy most deeply was:

_____

_____

_____

The turning point came when (your name) stopped worrying so much about what others thought and believed and began living his / her dream of becoming a person who:

_____

_____

_____

STEP 3

Practice the following process faithfully, staying ever-focused on what you discover at the bottom of your dig. What would be a more natural life for you, that you discovered from seeking an opportunity to life your dreams?

These pages are designed to bring about a means of rebuilding your story, beginning with clearing away any surface story you tell yourself that has been getting in your way to go deeper into your inner landscape. It is here that you to get your focus back on track. Doesn't it make a whole lot more sense to remove your energy and time from those thoughts and activities which do not align with what you really care about, and match up your attention with what makes life worth living? No one's saying you have to drop everything by yesterday. All I'm saying is that if you developed more faith in what brings you joy and excitement, life would be a whole lot juicier. Another way of saying this is: what if what you were seeking was also seeking you?

Does taking your own hidden dreams seriously mean dropping everything? No! It means making only those choices which support that for which your heart is longing. Life need not be so black and white as the monkey mind (ego) tries to make it appear. What this does mean is experimenting a tiny bit each day with shifting your decision-making function from mostly your head's little monkey mind to your heart's innate Wisdom. To do so means tossing out the clutter, the dirty diapers, so to speak, in the way of reaching your internal diamond. Where you are digging is the right place to make contact with your dream.

Note: But doing this doesn't mean that you've got to park your brain at the door. You've got a good brain. It is important to learn the skillset required to use your fine mind as a servant to your heart. They are meant to be buddies, after all. Most likely, skills you have learned earlier will be useful. In Part 3, Framing, you will meet Maggie. Maggie's career as a landscape architect and arborist, for example, became helpful when she began her vocation as a quilter

What follows in the next chapter must be used consistently over time to produce the best results. I'm drawing on the Great Truths discovered by Wisdom Teachers who come from every culture. Using it over time has produced amazing shifts in my own story, I can tell you, and likewise in the stories of those people I've shared it with from every continent, who have committed to the practice. What you read will be simple but is not easy. It's not easy because you must practice! Your monkey mind wants to distract you. Your monkey mind is the seducer extraordinaire, hopping from this branch to the next with its thoughts of 'to dos, regrets, shoulds, ought tos, comparisons, judgments, fears, opinions, and if onlys! This ego state will do anything to throw you off the scent of what brings spontaneous joy. Remember, it's "thou shalt" thoughts that dissipate your focus and steal away your life! They are what must be cleared away from your surface identity to build a heart-led life. Returning then to who you are beneath mental monkey chatter will work to change your story and change your life! Are you ready? Fasten your seatbelt.

CHAPTER 9

Prescribed Practice for Greater Clarity

Let's begin. Do not do the following while you are driving or operating equipment. This is your time just for you; it's your chance to focus only on what is within.

Now, find a place where you can relax, let go, and shift your focus from "out there" to what's within. Let whoever needs to be notified know that you are 'in conference' and cannot be disturbed. I strongly recommend that you read and record the following in your voice or have someone read it to you slowly. That way, the flow will not be interrupted.

With a softened focus, read/record slowly what follows, pausing to close your eyes as needed. Now, lay down the burden that has brought you here.

Just breathe . . . . You are entering the storyline for your freedom that will promote ease in your system . . . . and joy in your heart . . . . Take your time . . . . All you need do is begin to rest now . . . . Don't worry if you drift off . . . . your unconscious mind will kick in and absorb whatever is needed . . . . and cultivate the seeds of growth required to bring about greater aliveness . . . . deeper peace . . . . moving you through that very situation you've believed is a problem . . . . You are freely turning over your focus on problems . . . . and enjoying the experience of receiving . .

. . of receiving a Greater Good, your Greater Good . . . . You are turning over your concerns to Creative Intelligence which is here for you, now . . . . which is always here for you . . . . Right this moment . . . .

You are enjoying ease . . . . for you are letting go of all distractions . . . . all distractions . . . . all tensions . . . . all challenges . . . . For they are nothing, ... not even a hiccup to Higher Intelligence, of which you are a part . . . .

Feel this Life Substance . . . . the Life Substance that flows through all living things . . . . Feel this Life Substance flowing through you . . . .passing through every tissue . . . . into every cell . . . . washing through you from the top of your head . . . . all the way down . . . . to the soles of your feet . . . . Feel it connecting you with the earth . . . . with the earth of this body . . . . Yes, come back to this Life Substance, responding to your faith in it . . . . and bringing you clarity, ... Ease . . . . healing . . . .

This Greater Good . . . . to which you are indelibly intertwined is bringing you the exact experience you desire . . . . the exact experience that your heart needs today . . . . For you are a reflection of Creation . . . .

You are relaxing into the vision of what your heart desires . . . . You are sinking into the Love of a Greater Universe . . . . breathing in this Greater Love . . . . this Greater Wisdom . . . . and releasing all distracting and self-critical thoughts . . . . You no longer need them . . . . You are releasing all these restrictive thoughts . . . .

Imagine you can see yourself on a long, long journey, beginning by clearing away all distractions on the surface of your life, and a portal opens into a lush, natural jungle, which you chose to enter safely . . . . knowing that something loving, kind and wise is seeking you . . . .

You are relaxing more and more deeply . . . . surrendering the need to change anyone else's path, anyone else's behavior, returning to your own heart, letting go of directing anyone else . . . . respecting that each person in your life is following their own way . . . . doing the best they can . . . .

Right now, you are opening to the knock on the door to your heart's deepest desire, trusting your heart . . . . trusting that your heart is a cell in a Greater Heart that unites all living things with Life Substance Itself . . . . Right now, you are hearing more deeply than ever before, that part of your nature which has always been with you . . . . even though you've believed it was gone forever . . . .

Right now, you are breathing in a Greater Peace, ... a Greater Harmony into the depths of who you are . . . . You are focusing beautifully on what is healing . . . . on what inspires, and lifts you up . . . . .Focusing on your connection to this breath . . . . .this breathing in . . . . this breathing out . . . . This gentle breeze of life passing through you.

  You are breathing in beautifully your connection to the Web of Life . . . . breathing in and out this energy . . . . which unifies you with all living things . . . .

You are resting in Bigger Hands you are a jewel in the Great Mother's heart A perfect expression of that which is beyond imagination, that which heals, and nourishes you . . . . always here, always believing in you . . . . always breathing Its Mysterious Life Substance through, animating you with its Wonder and Mystery . . . . You are resting in Bigger Hands . . . . and resting in a Greater Good . . . . releasing all striving . . . . all 'efforting'.

You are realizing a Greater Blueprint that is harmonious with your heart, for your life . . . . slipping into the steady support of a Bigger Story of which you are a part Resting now, relaxing in the natural great peace . . . . your exhausted mind . . . . finding peace . . . . entering the Stillness in which a far more beautiful world than you've ever met . . . . opening itself to you now and you are breathing in and breathing out . . . . knowing in your heart that you are approaching the Centerpoint of your True, most Natural you . . . . your innermost Truth that is here to wisely guide your very next footsteps along more joyful, peaceful . . . . purposeful lines . . . . You do not have to figure these footsteps out

. . . . just content yourself with dwelling in this limitless, unending Love . . . . unifying with the Source of who you are . . . . your Greater, Best . . . . most Authentic . . . . flowing . . . . focused Self . . . .

Nothing to figure out, just a simple, softening . . . . dropping into that space which is your heart . . . . your magnificently constructed heart which is here for you . . . . beating and resting without any strain whatsoever on your part . . . . Breathing in this Life Substance, denying yourself no longer the healing balm in the Great Stillness . . . . Nothing you must do or achieve here . . . . for while you have thoughts, you are more than your thoughts . . . . While you have a body . . . . you are more than your body . . . . In this space, in this Stillness . . . . you are shown the radiant Light . . . . the Truth of who you most naturally are . . . .

In this sacred space and time, you ask the Stillness: What is the truth of my heart right now? And you rest, now, in the knowing that anything else need not concern you . . . . for you sense your birthright . . . . your Original Place and Way of Belonging to this Greater Love which allows your little monkey mind to rest itself . . . . so that you are left free to receive the Love, the Wisdom . . . . the guidance to create the story that you wish to live out today . . . . A story without limitations, distractions, mental prison cells You relax in the knowing that the goal of your heart is not impatient . . . . you relax in the knowing that the desire in your heart is kindness, ... is courteous to who you are . . . . never straining . . . . never critical . . . . always allowing always inviting . . . . always encouraging . . . . your belongingness to this Universe . . . .

Your story is unfolding beautifully . . . . .for it is based upon sim-plicity . . . . It is based upon ease . . . . It is based upon the Truth of the most natural, creative you . . . . which you are only just beginning to get the tiniest little inkling ofYou are relaxing into and savor-ing trusting that Life Force supports your freedom to express who you

really are . . . . Here you are free to be you Here, receiving the nourishing you've been needing from the Spirit of Life, now . . . . and forever
flowing through you . . . . .as you are focusing on deep rest . . . . enjoying
the Dance of new life . . . . Eternal Life expressing Itself through you . .
. . abundantly, joyously . . . . Creatively . . . . breathing in an expanding
sense of Purpose and Place . . . . releasing all need to stress and strain .
. . . relaxing into a deep and abiding patience . . . . uncovering your own
Pearl of Wisdom, baby step by baby step, for this is how you grow your
story in the best possible and organic way.

Imagine now a quilt of many squares. Pretend there is one square
before you which pictures your joy that is seeking you. Pretend this
square of your life quilt shows a picture of you in a creative relationship with life that brings deep satisfaction. Rest in this scene,
knowing that joy is seeking you as you give yourself permission to
let your heart wisdom guide you more. You are resting in knowing
you are most Beloved, greatly cherished as an instrument of Creative
Intelligence . . . . an expression of Divine Beauty, and Infinite Wisdom
at work in the world through this form called you . . . .

You are needed as you are . . . . perfectly, joyfully . . . . gratefully
attuned to your most natural self . . . . Imagining your Best Self alive
and well in the world today . . . . Imagining your deepest, most trea-
sured being expressing itself in bold and confident ways in that very
situation where you've been hesitating to be yourself. . . . . Imagining
yourself expanding your natural self's confidence . . . . more freely,
creating the story of your own Best Life today . . . . Imagining yourself breaking through that self-limiting way of seeing yourself you
no longer need . . . . Imagining living out your day in ways which
make your heart happy . . . . Imagining your exhausted mind at last
resting in the Natural Great Peace . . . . Imagining yourself revising
your story of who you are, expanding your lungs . . . . moving more
and more freely through the minutes flowing like a river . . . . in the
most natural, powerful and nourishing way.

Feel the River of Life flowing through you now . . . . setting you free to enjoy the revised story of who you came here to be, in the world today . . . . imagining yourself completely free to be who you are most naturally . . . . moving with ease . . . . hope . . . . aliveness.

. . . . This is Who You are . . . . Right here . . . . and Right Now . . . . And so, it is . . . .

Taking a nice deep cleansing breath…gently opening your eyes softening your focus…coming back into the room…

Record your experience, dating it with the day and year. Do this consistently for the next six weeks, with at least one continuing experience that week. Six weeks from now, reread what you've experienced and how your thoughts about your story are beginning to shift and expand, assuming a revised version of your life in process of growth.

Caution:

As you move through the next six weeks, be patient with yourself! Your monkey will try to slip into your process, and seduce you away from your process, because the very idea of a revised way of being in the world is threatening to your ego. As you observe yourself slipping into old patterns that pull you back into the mental prison cell, keep in mind the bigger picture, suggesting that who you really are is forever searching for a creative way to express its best, most truthful, greater good.

Your Life Quilt from Significant Experiences

To integrate these observations, make your own paper life quilt. Draw a large box. Now, divide it evenly into nine squares using two vertical lines and two horizontal lines.

Choose a "square" of your imaginary life quilt. Doodle (or write) an image that best captures what came to you during the guided imagery exercise.

The more senior you are, the more such events you have had. For the younger participants, go easy on yourself. There is much more clarity to discover unifying threads in your life story quilt.

> . . . . the experience of the deepest Self is so enlivening that it seeks some sort of local activity and motion. This consciousness has intent. Pure motion is not enough. It is, rather, a progressive expression of itself, as from plant life came before animals, and animals before people. But this is not the endpoint of Spirit expressing Itself, we know of the mineral, plant, animal, and human kingdoms. But we do not know how Spirit will express itself next. Each progression has led . . . . toward the development of a more perfect Individuality and therefore . . . . we may reasonably infer that the next step will take us still further in the same direction. We want something more perfect than we have yet reached, but our ideas as to what it should be are various.
> Judge Thomas Troward

CHAPTER 10

Arriving at the Edge

The fact is that we cannot advance our human story without a major shift in focus. Consider the homeowner who has lived in his house for decades and accumulated many memories. But a flood comes through the sliding glass door, creating toxic mold everywhere. Nothing can be done except to tear down the walls and collapse his home. At first, he is distraught. What is to become of him? How can he live without the previous shelter? No answers come. First, he must accept there is no going back to what was before. He must take a leap into the unknown and deal with his broken-heartedness. What was is no longer.

The next level of advancing psycho-spiritually in this lifetime requires evolving from the head-based human to the fifth brain: the heart-based human, meaning living our lives in an awakened relation with all beings. Each of us must play our part. That said, shifting from lives "of quiet desperation," where our monkey minds are going a million miles a minute, filled with angst about tomorrow, to lives that are heart-based and calm, does not happen overnight or by magical thinking. Nor does the shift happen without sacrifice. The aforementioned story required the homeowner to accept what once had been his home was gone.

Yes, this metaphor is true for each of us on the cusp of unexpected and unwanted experiences. We try like the dickens to hang on tight to what once was. We might hear cries from the distance which shout: 'just let go.' Easier said than done. We are cling-ons, grasping for what once was. Living whole-heartedly will not allow it. We must let go.

Change requires us to endure desert times, where we feel dry, empty, lost, fallow, and empty-handed. Where once stood your psychological 'house,' now there is only dirt. These are the times when you find yourself standing, metaphorically, on the Edge of the abyss, miles from what was once familiar and even comfortable. Picture it as follows:

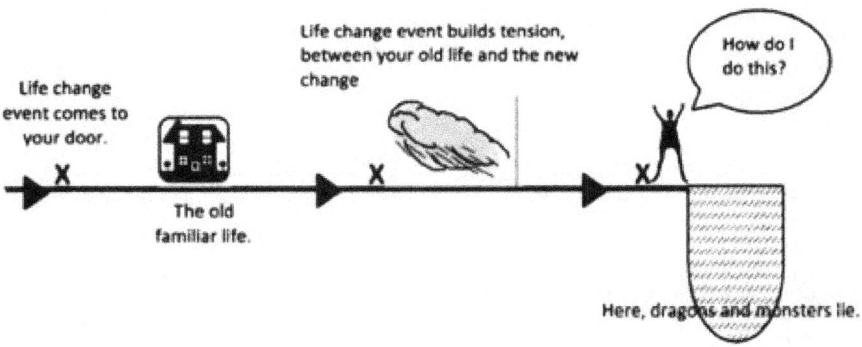

When you come to your own Edge, you are forced to face who you are in the absence of your props, in the absence of your carefully-manicured old picture of who you are and determine what you truly need. At the Edge, we stand on the brink of discovery, but not before we face our relationship to the void. This is tricky business, as old ways begin to unravel.

What Happens at the Edge?

Edges lead into unknown territory, which is what makes them so gosh-darn scary. Just yesterday, a professional man with some degree of fame and accomplishment asked me if I had ever been afraid when leaping into a reshaping of my career. I laughed. "Terrified, is more like it," I told him.

Are you kidding? At the moment of that leap, all signs of a safety net vanish. Taking that leap meant leaving behind really good friends and the career I would have done for nothing. I loved it that much. The last thing I expected when I met my own son's sudden, traumatic death was that this would so radically change my life and world view about pretty much everything. All I knew at that moment, and in the days to come, was that I did not know how my heart could possibly go on beating. I was at my Edge. I was called to this Edge. I was afraid. Horrified. Same deal when my husband of over 40 years had to move into senior care due to his Parkinson's disease. We each had to dig our way through that gaping hole and go on living as best we could.

But, my friend, beyond that edge lives the true calling that is waiting for us. Believe it or not, what is waiting for you and me will be rejuvenating, restorative, and for some, even Sacred. No one will take such a leap unless they are deeply attuned to their own deepest Wisdom, which some call intuition. Daring to cultivate our intuition is possible only if our foundation is built on solid ground; if we are willing to accept, as long as necessary, empty hands and broken hearts. Unfortunately, whenever we go astray, we must return to our real foundation again and again. To do so means putting up with tearing down the old to reach terra firma.

Something I should mention here is that there are edge seasons. For some, there is the sense of life becoming so cold, so emptied; we can compare this state to the starkness of winter and its icy edges. For others the spring-oriented leap might be a promise of renewed life, of the budding of new possibilities. The third variety might be compared to summer, where the leaper does so because the promise of life's blooming can be enough to send them over the edge. Then, again, when signs of life decay appear, there is no way to go except over the edge.

Blessedly, even the greatest Masters have had their bouts, so I took solace: Jesus, 40 days in the Wilderness, The Buddha, 40 days beneath the Bodhi tree, Moses, 40 years wandering out there in the hinterlands with his people. And me, years and years of wandering, seeking, getting lost then found, then lost, trying to Braille out my own way through the forest; trying this structure, only to shed what wasn't real for me; trying to eke out that internal structure that required integration when I could not yet find the map. This is how we meet our Edges. If you can remember that the experience is encountered by the greats, and the common, as a part of human development, it helps. That way, we take the whole thing less personally! That is how we need to frame our edges, because the process of natural growth is impersonal. Nature cannot evolve without discarding what has grown lifeless.

Here's a piece which states it beautifully:

"Come to the edge," he said.
They said, "We are afraid."
"Come to the edge," he said.
They came.
He pushed.
And they flew.

–Christopher Logue

When we stand at the Edge, we draw back, big time. And, why not? If you are wise, you surrender, breathe deeply, and trust that mysterious "Something" that's greater than your fear. You are wise to ask for help from that which is greater than your old identity. If you do not knock, how can the door be opened?

Growing Forward

What this all gets down to is the real challenge. You discover what you need to surrender in order to grow (yes, grow) forward. You must surrender your fear. We must surrender every blessed excuse that holds us smaller than we are. You must surrender your story that you'll never get through this pass of pain. You must surrender your belief in short cuts. Groan.

Edges are no place for the starry-eyed, for their task is vigorously and practically applying spiritual principles in everyday life. This does not mean you must either be religious or adhere to dogma. What is required is acceptance that the Spirit of Life moves through you, as it does all nature, with an urge toward growth. You cannot expand without edges. Nor can I. They are our growing places where there's the chance to awaken, to live freely out loud, to accept that solid cornerstones must be laid to support a richer life.

Why is the Edge necessary? Jung said it so well: Who looks outside dreams; Who looks inside awakens.

When we are faced with a big enough Edge, the loss of something crucial to our heart and identity, jumping into the Unknown confronts you and me with our personal dragons (limited thinking). But, as Jung quipped, "When you are falling, you might as well jump." In other words: become intentional. It's far more attractive than whining! But, if you must whine for a while or throw a hissy fit, that's okay, too. Just remember, the sand is slipping through the hourglass.

"Descent" Original illustration (in color) by Cara Barker, 1991

Resisting the Edge

When you resist your present Edge that requires you to expand, you resist life, falling out of relatedness to it. Think back to a time something was changing in your life and you resisted too long and paid a price. All stress comes from resistance to life 'as is.' Fill in the following:

When (circle your current condition: divorce, loss, discouragement, an unexpected move, financial problems, career upset, changes in health, etc.)

_____

_____

_____

Was changing my life, I pretended that:

_____

_____

_____

And resisted the change by telling myself the story that:

_____

_____

_____

The price I paid for avoiding and fully facing my Edge, alone, for as long as it took, and coming to terms with this life change was:

_____

_____

_____

The lesson I learned and need to remember now is:

_____

_____

_____

So that I can be free to:

_____

_____

_____

Meeting the Edge happens when we realize that we're not running the show. An Edge well met liberates us to metaphorically rise from a well-grounded foundation and begin the work of facing what feels like emptiness. Until then, we are, as Hew Len puts it, displaced people.

In my own Edge which displaced me, involving the death of my son, I was faced with the necessity of surrendering my usual action plan. Normally, and historically (not unlike the high-achieving women I interviewed in my ten-year study: World Weary Woman: Her Wound and Transformation, when loss pushed me to my own Edge, I got busy. Distracting myself with whatever person, place, or thing would occupy my attention so I didn't have to face the void. Normally, I avoided facing my relationship with absence. My ego had its own stomping of feet. "This is not what I planned! This is not where I was supposed to be. This is someone else's story on Oprah, not mine."

When you're falling, you might as well jump.

Carl G. Jung

Unmet Edges have a way of gathering momentum until you face what my childhood friend named Martha called "the biggie." Here, there's nowhere left to run. In my case, I did not know that there was something I'd fled for a lifetime that didn't catch up with me until my boy was in his grave. I'd been avoiding dealing with my unfinished business from my childhood—times of profound loneliness so frightening that I hid them from myself. But this time I could not run: the loneliness produced a search to find an inner belonging and for interior affection and love, because there was no solace in the external that could heal this ache. I'd spent too many years trying to find what I wanted 'out there': a search to find 'my tribe,' the futile attempt of turning myself into a pretzel to find 'them,' to please 'them.' When I'd come to this recognition before, at other big Edges, I ran away, terrified that if I met the Edge, I'd get sucked down into the pain of the undertow and never surface for air. I kept running from it until my son, Matt, died. Then there was no place left to run. It was time to make a leap of faith. It was time to jump into the very thing I'd feared: the dark emptiness. I reached the spot on my path where I knew I just had to give up running away from my demon: the Great Loneliness and fear of vulnerability. It was time to get real and to tell myself the truth; to surrender all façade of the old "I'm fine" persona when I was anything but.

We are displaced people wandering aimlessly in the desert of our minds. . . . Resistance keeps us in a constant state of anxiety and spiritual, mental, physical, financial, and material impoverishment.

Dr. Hew Len

Those who've been consciously on their own journey know what I mean when I talk about the endless hours of hiding from ourselves. Listen to the words of Susan L. Taylor:

> . . . with my many fears tenuously contained, I greeted the world each day buffed and polished . . . my clothing, hair, nails, and makeup all impeccably done, and no one seemed to notice the cracks lengthening beneath the façade of cheerfulness I wore like armor. I became so skilled at the masquerade that even I began to believe it was real.

We can get so good at packaging that we can lose ourselves in the conspiracy of acting real when we are being false. What was it that Will Shakespeare said? "To thine own self be true."

The good news is that once you and I are brave enough to face the truth that we are not our packaging , we can revise our story along much more authentic lines! The subject of getting real, the art of authenticity, is so vital that it is one of the four essential cornerstones you must lay if you are serious about coming home to your best self whose source is Love. Who's ready for more good news? If so, turn the page.

CHAPTER 11

Separating Fact from Fiction

Are you open to good news? Our path is always self-correcting. If our old metaphorical house is beyond repair, best to face it squarely, and let the old go, prepare to begin anew by digging deeper to who we really are most naturally. My friends and colleagues in Taiwan refer to the surprises that help us course correct as the "Greater Arrangement." Around the world, increasing numbers of people are recognizing the truth of the joke: "If you want to make God laugh, show Him your plans!"

Susan Taylor puts this clearly:

> The path I'd been following wasn't the right one for me. . . . I had chosen what was attractive and what I'd been taught was safe, but not what was true for me.

This resonates with me. How many times I've come up against this one. Particularly in the corporate world, both here and abroad, there's a limit to how genuine you can be. For example, it may be in vogue to say the four-letter word that starts with 's' and ends with 't', but not okay to say the other four-letter "s" word: Soul. Some years ago, a CEO told me "It won't market well. People won't buy it, so forget it. You cannot say the word "Soul" anymore in teaching."

I had this challenge when someone told me to just ignore my

truth and 'go with the program,' adding, 'don't fight the company way.' That's why I left a high-paying, multi-perk position, one which I loved more than any job before. We can compromise many things, but not our Truth; not if we want to be free. Removing yourself from any false way of living means something dies. Mostly, what must go is the fictional story you have believed about what's possible for you. Most retreat, too fearful of this sort of dying. Maybe that's why the words Shakespeare penned long ago hold true today:

To thine own self be true.

William Shakespeare

The fact is that we are even more afraid of 'full-on' living than we are of dying. We're afraid it will cost too much. This is one of the teachings of the Edge. Letting go means death of the old and just doing what your heart tells you that you must and dealing with the fallout later. Simply put, we must get gutsy.

This doesn't make it easy, though. When I left behind the seduction of company benefits and rich good times with buddies, this decision threatened my beliefs about security. Ironically, by doing the very thing that was forbidden, to teach my own way, in my own offering, on my own terms, with considerable risk, security was relocated where it could not be reduced ever again: inside. You cannot come home to your own Truth without cutting the ropes that bind you to false moorings. You will never set sail to your freedom trail until you celebrate more self-compassion.

By the way, the first business I designed, called 'Crossroads,' failed. Embarrassing, yes. Yet it did give me the painful feedback that I was at my own crossroads and needed to dig deeper in my life, having just remarried to a widower with three teenage daughters not so thrilled about having a stepmother. Archetypes arise during times of unexpected change. Relationships are not always pretty until we are brave enough to meet one another beneath assumptions, disappointments, and projections. Despite that unspeakable pain for us all, I am grateful. The experience shoved me into my own Jungian Analysis, where I learned about the power of archetypes. Said my wise analyst, "Don't presume others know who we really are when an archetype arises, such as stepmother. Archetypes are so powerful that they can override the truth. Best to not take archetypal conflicts personally."

Now, that was worth the money spent!

Fighting Edges

It's ironic, isn't it, we resist the very thing that can usher in a joyous homecoming for us. I'd spent a lifetime trying to wallpaper over a spiritual nature to fit in, be liked, and be well-paid. But in the end, bringing forward what I'd been hiding liberated my life. My way was neither the church dogma way nor the corporate way of playing safe and legislating the lives of others. My way was to find and trust my own path, from what *was* into what *could be*, by crossing over the Edge. The fact is, that what makes Edges so intimidating is that they bring us to the frontier of the unknown and unknowable.

To get from where you are to where you want to be, begin by facing the facts. Where are the deadened places in your life? Write them down here:

Remember the advice Jesus gave his followers following guideline at their own Edge:

Let the dead bury the dead.

Why did the Master Teacher tell us all to let go of that which lacks life? As long as we hang on to what is lackluster, we are going against the river of who we are and what specifically came here to become, offer, and serve. Crazy, huh? But maybe not, because we are only human resisting the fear that would otherwise bring the renewal of life that is seeking us. We simply cannot expand our self-concept that this process requires without surrendering to reinvention after clearing the land of what has been.

Edges as Reinvention

We live in a state of constant reinvention. Your GI tract reinvents itself every three to five days, and adult skin, around every thirty days. At a cellular level, you are continuously reinventing your body. This very moment, now, you are in the act of becoming. The question is: Who are you becoming? Rumi put it beautifully: We have no idea what we are.

Most of us have no idea of who we are at the core level because we look at ourselves but do not see who's opposite the mirror. We each guard against change. Our knees tremble. What to do? Not to worry. Listen to Rumi's suggestion:

Keep walking though there's no place to get to.
Don't try to see through the distances.
That's not for human beings. Move within.
But don't move the way fear makes you move.

Let me repeat: ". . . don't move the way fear makes you move."

Prepare to be misunderstood. You need to rise up, speak up, get relevant. Practice saying to yourself and others: "Here is where I am. This is where I stand," even if your way of expressing yourself seems corny or cuckoo to others. Who cares? At the end of your life, no one will stand in for you on your deathbed.

Until we bring into balance our activities and our capabilities, we will feel the frustration of working against life. . . . The frustration we feel from not realizing our potential isn't a punishment but a blessing, a self-correcting mechanism.

Susan Taylor

It's time to grow up, get up, step out, and strut your stuff. You cannot find the answer to why you are really here in this crazy, life pretending to be less than who you are, any more than you can come home through magical thinking. The vast majority of the millions who've read Napoleon Hill's classic *Think and Grow Rich* have not become rich because of unwillingness to expand their self-concept and take persistent, consistent, and manageable daily action steps in the direction of their chief aim in life. The same thing holds true for most lottery winners who lose their big winnings. Neither you nor I will ever enrich our lives by childlike thinking that prefers fiction to fact.

We think our happiness comes from our toys. Maybe God is trying to push us out of the nursery, and get us to grow up.

C.S. Lewis

What's beautiful is as you surrender the fictional you and take up the journey toward authenticity in earnest, you find your real tribe. Sir Laurens van der Post was one of mine. The first white man to rise up against apartheid in Africa, he went on to inspire people around the world. At eight years old, as a white boy raised in South Africa, he realized that for 300 years his ancestors had dishonored the Bushmen. And so, he put on his little suit and coerced his nanny to take him to the tribal chief, where he sought forgiveness and pledged to make right the wrongs of his people. He left the nursery and followed his Call. Those of us who knew him, and have read his works, are forever grateful for what he found. We are not alone. I told him at dinner one night in Zurich that one of my favorite stories he ever wrote was:

> I found myself thinking of a Sindakwena saying: 'The journey makes the stranger at dawn a neighbor beside the fire at night.'

Unless you are willing to tell yourself the truth and own up to the fact that you are more than what you express, your journey will be stalled by pretending. Until you set out on a fact-based journey, you will never meet others on theirs.

Listen to one of my favorite author, Sue Monk Kidd, who describes, so truthfully, the beginning of the urge toward growth:

> Believe me, I wanted to shove all this away and pretend it didn't exist. But I couldn't. Life tasted of cardboard and smelled of stagnant air. At times I found myself shut in a closet of pain, unable to find the door. In my blackest moments I actually fantasized about running away from home to find the vital part of me that I had lost.

Finding your true path and purpose requires letting go. It is in this darkness of the forest, the wild, that growth takes place. It is not accidental that so many enduring stories having to do with homecoming contain forest scenes, such as Hansel and Gretel. "We get lost, we struggle," said my teacher, Marie-Louise von Franz.

Edges are times to re-write our lives. This is fact, not fiction. Whether Jesus is one of your teachers or not, what he said "holds water."

"Go sell what you have . . . and follow me."

Mark 10:21

Director-Producer Tom Shadyrac points out in his documentary titled *I AM* that nature never takes more than it needs. Applying this principle to his own life, Shadyrac radically rewrote his life from excess to simplicity. I am in process of doing likewise. It is difficult but liberating. Sometimes, the rewrite begins in captivity. Take the great writer, O'Henry, for example. It was not until he was totally broke and imprisoned that he met his own 'unlived life' and began to write from a part of himself he had never before met. Crisis has a way of expanding our self-concept if we are willing to let go.

Napoleon Hill, whose work have sold over 15 million copies around the world, long before the advent of the internet, wrote the following from what was discovered as thematic from the most prosperous men:

> Remember that all who succeed in life get off to a bad start and pass through heartbreaking struggles before they 'arrive.' The turning point in the lives of those who succeed usually comes at the moment of some crisis, through which they are introduced to their 'other selves'.

We continue to see ourselves the way we always have until it no longer works. O'Henry saw himself as the product of misfortune until he was incarcerated and found his voice. Jesus's disciples 'saw' themselves as fisherman and other laborers until they met their teacher and were asked to go out into the world and "Let your Light shine."

This does not mean that the process happens overnight or that we comprehend the greater story right away. For example, when I wrote *World Weary Woman: Her Wound and Transformation*, I believed, after a ten-year study, that it was the shared experience of loss that prompted the successful women in it to achieve. But this was not the whole story. Years later, with more experience, I discovered that the underlying shared issue was that each of those achieving, producing individuals were catapulted into a journey that forced them to enter a relationship with absence, without their beloved.

They faced a void. In the hole, they found what they least expected: the Whole. The Whole within the hole became their bedrock; their gravitas on which they took their stand. They'd been to hell and back and knew it. In other words, they learned to organize around their relationship with absence in creative ways, albeit unconsciously, which required dealing with suffering.

Who would I be if I stopped trying to manage all this? Where's the room for me? Is there room for me?

Sue Monk Kidd

We either come to be part of the problem or part of the solution. We either repeat the old litany, our gospel of despair, or sing with awe as we welcome the new sunrise. If you asked people in your circle, would they say that you privately sing a dirge or a song of awe? Why not ask? You might be surprised by their answers.

CHAPTER 12

The Necessity of Sorting

Why would we bother?

We keep journals or write diaries because our stories not only need to be told, but they also need to be heard, even if it's by the pages of our private work for our eyes only. Writing down our stories helps us sort things out. I began my own journal with colored pencils, not unlike so many women everywhere who felt the inner urge. My biggest fear, like that of many others, was that it would be found by unwanted eyes, and then my truth, my heartaches, and hopes would be prematurely "outed." The need grew stronger for me to begin the process of writing regularly in a journal in the 1970s, when I began to read May Sarton's journals and later, Madeleine L'Engle's. Their truths were so unvarnished it began to haunt me. (If you haven't read them, consider this treat.) Their wise words prompt essential questions.

What does it mean to have a voice with such depth? What would it take to find and own my own story; to really come home to it? I began in earnest, frightened I'd find nothing. But something else known well by all the May Sartons and Madeleine L'Engles spurred me on. In 1981, I urged my mother to author her own story. Despite resistance to recording her own "pearls of wisdom" on her deathbed, she did so, and found it healing.

Nine months later, as I read her words after her funeral, a part of her I'd never known came to life. Her words were lovely, vulnerable, soft-hearted, philosophical, and sweet. Here's one excerpt:

> *When I came to Chicago from our small Finn village on the border, I was stunned that first night by all the bright lights in the big city. There were no cows mooing in the pasture, no chickens scratching from the coop. No, here in the big city, I was completely alone. Would I become one of the chickens scratching my way out? I had no idea what would become of me. All I knew was I was here, and my people were far away. I would need to make the best of it, ready or not. And yet, there was this deep down hope that maybe here I'd find my very own life . . . my own way in this world.*

Her first week working at the Chicago hospital was the night of the Saint Valentine's Massacre. I imagine my young mom facing all the mutilated Al Capone mob being carried into emergency, where she was working that night. After which, she wrote:.

> *The way home to who I really am involves a willingness to release the familiar, the comfortable, and set out on my own, regardless the cost.*

I began to sense that, like my mother, I too had a story to tell. For the record, so do you. While the last thing I believed about myself was that I would become a writer, something deeper than my monkey mind insisted on leaving behind a true record; a true record that digs to the very core of who we are. In short order, I came across May Sarton and others, but May was first. May Sarton's (1912-95) journals opened the door to me on the importance of recording experience and human relationships as a woman really lives and feels them, even if she doesn't say so aloud with a microphone. In the beginning, I couldn't believe how mundane Sarton's journals were, filled to the brim with everyday events of discouragements and hope, visiting neighbors, pets' antics, worries and dreams, recipes, and anxieties. But what was even more surprising to me was that somehow these tiny, original details were oddly captivating to the 'underground me' who'd been at risk of being swallowed up like Jonah, only in my case, in the corporate whale. May spoke to my inner Jonah who wanted to live and to come home to a better life, a deeper love, and purpose for my life.

Prescription and Treatment

Find a quiet place to nourish your body and Soul and do so. Then do the following practice:

Imagine your life as it is today and notice that pocket where all is not yet perfect. Now, imagine ten years from now and nothing whatsoever has changed except you are ten years older in a world that's ten years further down the road. How does this experience make you feel?

_____

_____

_____

_____

Now, pretend that it is ten years in the future, and out of the darkest area of your present challenge (name it) comes tremendous beauty, wisdom, love, and prosperity. Imagine yourself flowing at full capacity in this exercise. Imagine yourself investing time and energy into some area that touches your heart and expands your life in a positive way that makes you feel fulfilled. How does this experience make you feel?

Today, my present challenge is:

_____

_____

_____

_____

The experience of 'flowing at full capacity' in my future would include the following:

Beauty flowing at full capacity in this area might look like:

_____

_____

_____

_____

Wisdom flowing at full capacity:

_____

_____

_____

_____

Love flowing at full capacity:

_____

_____

_____

_____

Prosperity and abundance flowing at full capacity:

_____

_____

_____

_____

Summary: We get to choose which path we take. Which do you prefer? Remember: we have to lose our life (ego construction) to find our life. We have to leave our little box to find our house of true belonging. If you refuse to leave the too-small nest, however, nature will conspire to shove you out to the edge. Ready or not, now is your time. No worries, though. What's on the next page will help.

CHAPTER 13

Returning Home:
The Prodigal in You

Regardless of whether our literal childhood home still stands or not, there is a familiar urge to bring who we really are to that home base. To come home to the full capacity of your innate gifts, capacities, and secret delights, you've got to start trusting yourself more and doubting your own authentic nature less. As long as you believe you are separate from what's sacred, that creative intelligence has nothing to do with you, it's impossible to relax. That's what keeps us on the hamster wheel, running like crazy to be other than we are. That's what keeps us fixated on possessions, stockpiling for that "rainy day." Mistrusting the future, we resist change.

But as we get older and enter life's afternoon, we try to fit into the clothes of the morning, but they are too tight. So, we've got to go back to our Original nature, trust it, and 'embrace it, rather than struggling against it. Do you live an inspired life? For me, to do so takes great empty spaces and much stillness to reconnect with the feeling that fuels creative inspirations.

Life is not about avoiding the storm. Life is about learning to dance in the rain.

Author unknown

As I told you earlier, for the past five summers, my own stillness and spaciousness came through broken bones to get me to stop running from what my Soul needed for nourishment and expression. What will it take for you, like the Prodigal, to return home to what delights and calms your heart? Think of this process as your own particular Love Project, which is another way of looking at your unfolding purposeful life.

Prescription

Secure some time to devote to your truth. Consider this question: what will it take for you to trust what most delights and calms your heart? More drama? More pain? More challenge? Let's get real. One of the most touching female writers, Anne Morrow Lindberg, suffered through the kidnapping and murder of her child before she wrote *Gifts from the Sea*. Challenge is not the enemy. In her own words, Anne tells us: Perhaps we never appreciate the here and now until it is challenged.

Maybe, like the Prodigal son, you simply awaken one morning, look around you, and know you can do better, get up, dust yourself off, and start moving in a better direction. And you might even find that you can still dance.

Ask yourself these questions:

What will it take for me to trust my heart more?

For example, maybe finding a buddy and agreeing to support one another to trust your heart in some specific way, perhaps contacting each other weekly when you are feeling hesitant might be one strategy. My dear sister-friend, Judith, and I do this on Monday nights, although we live miles apart. We call this our 'tea party.' What are other strategies that appeal to you?

_____

_____

_____

_____

What would calm my heart more?

For example, you might want to practice meditation or yoga or take a daily walk through nature. What would calm your heart?

_____

_____

_____

_____

What would truly delight my heart more?

For example, maybe there's an old friend you have not seen in a long time and a visit or a phone call are in order. Maybe, some time in the garden or by the seashore are in order, or even gathering beautiful paint chips to redo a drab room in your home and you have been wanting to change for ages. Maybe sitting and doing absolutely nothing would delight you. Or a class. What some strategies you can use to maximize your own delight?

_____

_____

_____

_____

CHAPTER 14

Improving Your Dig

Your next step on the path home to the you that exists beyond a limited self-concept begins with self-honesty. Identify the constantly-looping thoughts that interrupt you from fully living. Maybe you've been waiting for divine intervention? Perhaps you've been holding a pity party? Magical thinking? Identify what's been holding you back.

_____

_____

_____

_____

Prescription

This week, identify the beliefs that are most limiting for you.

For example, "The reason I can't do what I want is that I don't know how to acquire the money and resources this would require."

Note that this self-limiting belief comes from not trusting. The 'how' is not your business. That will come. Your job is neither to figure out the 'how' nor the 'when.' Your job is to identify the 'what' that is your desire. Start here by identifying what limits you in your thinking:

_____

_____

_____

_____

_____

_____

Now imagine telling yourself a better story. Here's my own story for reference:

I'm no longer waiting but am diving into a vibrant, joyful, creative, connected life. I'm painting my story, writing my story, sharing my stories. I'm dancing my story, singing my stories. I'm playing, having a ball, having the time of my life, free of distracting myself with things I don't want to do and with people who won't solve their own problems. I'm freely living spontaneously, and prospering like never before. Whoopee! I'm creating a series of books and Audibles. I'm creating Love Projects. This next volume of my life is the flourishing creative artist alive in the world creating fresh new pieces of art! Cross-culturally, through heart-warming collaboration with people I just love! Oh yes, it is all abundantly funded!

Now, write out yours. Get some exclamation marks in it!

_____

_____

_____

_____

_____

_____

CHAPTER 15

A Better Story Means the Unexpected

As you move in the direction of expansion, there will be a zone that will surprise you, just like Juan's crew. Here's something I hope you, too, find helpful. Anatole France, as recorded in William Bridges's *Managing Transitions: Making the Most of Change*, puts it accurately:

> All changes, even the most longed for, have their melancholy, for what we leave behind us is a part of ourselves; we must die to one life before we can enter another.

Not to worry, then, when you pick up your metaphorical 'backpack' and head for your own metaphorical home with this better story than your monkey mind has told you is possible. You, too, might find melancholy nipping at your heels for a bit. Anatole France is right: it is normal. But for those raised with Western thinking, *particularly* Americans, this seems counter intuitive. During transition, I've had literally thousands of people tell me: "There must be something wrong. I'm moving forward in my life yet find myself feeling down at times. What's wrong?"

The answer is nothing. You are right on schedule, just like the freshly-emerging gooey butterfly who must depart the cocoon, all damp, and having never flown before. It struggles. It does not feel comfortable in its new-and-improved body. It requires warmth, space, and patience. So do we. In this in-between space, which Buddhists call the Bardo, we are in between worlds, not yet fully arrived as a hybrid.

I love how Sara Lawrence-Lightfoot puts it: "This is the space where the loss and liberation get negotiated."

Old habits must go.

> (William Bates) claims that in our highly mobile society where change and ambition are considered the coin of the realm, people fail to recognize that any transition process—in life, in love, in work—not only requires adapting to a new situation, but it also means letting go of old habits.

Prescription

Take time now to consider and ask yourself what old habits will you miss as you move forward and take on a way of expressing your Authentic Self that is expanding to accommodate more Love, more Wisdom? For example, maybe you'll miss what seemed routine before your move, literally or figuratively. When my own evolution required that we sell our home and move across the water, I missed my neighbors, friends, coffee haunts, grocery store, gym around the corner, favorite bookstore, and easy commute. I missed my assumption that we'd live in our familiar home forever. I missed my garden. I missed this identity, so predictable, like an old friend. I missed my assumptions, which are like familiar old shoes. That was two moves ago. Same process. Same distress.

Now it's your turn. What might you miss about your familiar narrative if you were to advance in the direction of your heart's deepest desire?

_____

_____

_____

_____

Integrating Change in Successful Ways

An amazing hybrid thinker by the name of Lewis Mehl-Madrona teaches material on this process from his own homecoming. In his case, Lewis was challenged to integrate his Western training as a physician with his ancestral roots as a medicine man. The result? His work is now focused on the business of creating healing narratives. Creating your own healing narrative is what we are doing here. Listen in to Lewis, who, like each of us Prodigals, has known success, setbacks, temporary melancholy, defeat, and forward movement.

> In the indigenous worldview . . . each person is the sum of all the stories that have been (or ever will be) told about him; the idea that our identity is formed from telling ourselves these stories leads us to realize that each person is unique and must discover how he will heal. No two people with the same diagnosis are narratively alike. All the stories are different. Treatments can't work if the stories we live have no place for healing.

A better narrative can begin in tiny ways. For instance, years ago, in 1981, I was walking to my practice past Seattle's Elliot Bay Bookstore. In the window was a print that, quite literally, stopped me in my tracks. The image was simple: a nomadic woman was walking east with a walking stick, her profile striking against the background. The colors were a combination of sunrise and sunset. She wore a striped shawl. An hour later at work, I was still obsessing over it. I thought of the image, one which was not my preferred artistic style at all. Yet throughout the day, I could not shake this "desert woman's" journey. Finally, I surrendered, went next door, and bought the thing. Nine months later, our lives took a dramatic turn. We moved to Colorado, at the base of the Rocky Mountains. I hung the portrait in our new home, which remained with us for twelve years until the movers lost it when we moved to the Arizona desert. One day, I realized that the woman in the picture was now alive in my life. We had come full circle. I no longer needed the painting. She was living inside my life. A brief time later she came to me in a meditation, and I sketched her portrait while in Europe. We were on the trek together by that time.

"It Has Begun" Original illustration (in color) by Cara Barker, 1991

When it is time to set out on our journey, the necessity has been seeded in us long before we put on our sandals and take the first step into the unfamiliar. Get ready. Get your house in order. The time is drawing near. It is no small wonder that the desert metaphor is used so often in transformation journeys. At a certain place in the road, when it is incumbent on you to grow or perish, something nudges you to set out into what's foreign and uncomfortable from necessity. That something is our very Soul. Witness Carl Jung's words from his famous *Red Book*, now released:

My Soul leads me into a desert of my own self. I did not think that my Soul is a desert, a hot, barren, desert without drink. The journey leads through hot sand, slowly wading without a visible goal to hope for? How eerie is this wasteland. . . . Why is my Soul a desert? Have I lived too much outside myself in men and events?

Carl Jung

Before he reached his inner desert, Jung had written over 20,000 letters to people he'd not met and published multiple books of depth. Now, if a creative genius like Swiss psychiatrist Carl Jung is surprised by his journey through the 'desert,' can we not cut ourselves some slack? We think we know ourselves until we are brave enough to step into the unknown, which strips us of all pretenses. We are moving into uncharted territory. This is why it is so helpful to take our dreams seriously enough to write them down and to reflect upon them with someone objective and who knows how to decode them. This is why it's so helpful to "hear" our body's symptoms and doodles as messengers. The psyche makes every attempt to help us course correct, but we must do our part and take what comes seriously. When we do this, our Life Force galvanizes and we move through stuckness.

Imagine that what is unfolding in your life is a work of art under-
derway. Out of chaos comes form, beauty, order.

Cara Barker

What stories do you suppose those Prodigals who make it through their metaphorical desert tell themselves? Lawrence-Lightfoot's research corresponds with my own published in 2001 (*World Weary Woman: Her Wound and Transformation*).

She reports:

> Each of the people I spoke to talks about new learning of this chapter as requiring a paradigm shift; many refer to the work as being integrative, a time to bring the pieces together, and make ourselves whole, to align our professed values with our actions, our rhetoric with our behaviors . . . . others discovering that the real struggles and insights during this transition are deeply spiritual . . . .

I know this to be so in my own "third chapter," where life required me to blend aspects of my nature into a revised composition if I were to advance in the most lively and authentic direction. Fortunately, those who have studied the process before me were a great assist, such as Mary Catherine Bateson, the daughter of Margaret Meade and Gregory Bateson. Her work, *Composing a Life*, drew a conclusion that women "come home" to who they are not in a linear fashion, but much like a quilter. As women, we live out our development in different "patches," which sooner or later must become integrated. In a more recent book, she wrote:

> One thing that you do in composing a life is to put together disparate elements that need to be in some kind of balance, like a still life with tools, fruit and musical instruments.

Lawrence-Lightfoot adds flesh to Bateson's bones by describing one such journey: *Grace's journey—from a place where she was well-known, respected, and deeply engaged, a place where her "layered life" to a place where she had no history, networks, or reputation—underscores the place of place; the shift in geography provokes new learning. First she feels the sting of loss—or status, identity, of all things familiar . . . Then, right on the heels of her sorrow, she sees the edge of her liberation from routines, rituals, and responsibilities of her old life. Extricating herself from ancient relationships, community expectations, and a life of service, she is transformed from being the mature mother nurturing and guiding her children, her younger colleagues at the press, her fellow activists, to being a 'gray-haired adolescent' making her way in a new town and beginning to find her way in a new career. Interestingly the freedom of not being known in her community and the infancy of her new vocation move her from the margins—a 'marginalization' that, in her eyes, gives her artistic voice legitimacy.*

I know exactly what she means. At thirty-nine years old, my husband and family moved to Boulder, Colorado. One day, standing at the crosswalk at Boulder Mall waiting for the light to turn green, something struck me like a lightning bolt. There, in my sweats, holding my little girl's hand, I was miles away from my former, very public life. At breakneck speed came the thoughts: no one knows who I am. I could be anything at all: a janitor, a florist, whatever. It doesn't matter. I was free. But I was also naked in terms of a very comfy persona.

What you and I are left to note in our changing stories of homecoming is that we must learn to hold the tension of opposites so that the new is born. No wonder we feel so vulnerable. We are free from the old, yet still hovering on the edge of the cocoon.

I can assure you that moving to an island, by way of example, does require navigating city fast with country slow until the new life rhythm arrives. You're smart to trust the process. Be forewarned, though: just as you think you've settled in, life can throw you a curveball. It has for me. But that's a story for another time and moving van!

Prescription

Truth time. Where have you been too impatient with yourself during your present transition?

_____

_____

_____

How does your impatience show up in your time management?

_____

_____

_____

How have you been unfair to yourself?

_____

_____

_____

Where might you benefit from self-forgiveness and self-compassion?

_____

_____

_____

What might this look like to others?

_____

_____

_____

CHAPTER 16

Digging Down Deep
Brings You Full Circle

One of the biggest myths spun from Human Development seminars and courses is that you can work out a core life issue once, and presto, it's gonzo. The fact is that these central issues are messengers moving us toward a continuing discovery of the essential hidden Self.

There are places to which you are called to revisit, maybe in different forms, but return to them you must if you genuinely want to become whole, authentic, and more radiantly, beautifully alive. And, when we face them squarely, the life energy which was stored up and wasted in these knots of unused life are liberated, and we experience a greater degree of aliveness. Some women that I met during my research for *World Weary Woman: Her Wound and Transformation* have described their process as symbolically gathering up the threads. In psychological terms, achieving this requires the deconstruction of beliefs about our unworthiness, lack, and victimization, and reconstruction of a self-concept that meshes with worthiness, deservingness, love, wisdom, abundance, prosperity, and well-being. As you make this choice, there is a decreasing inclination for pity parties, gossip, and seeing the glass as half empty. Instead, there is an increase in gratitude, resilience, receptivity, open-mindedness, and service. But be forewarned: the process takes the time it takes.

There's nothing like times of loss or discouragement to remind us of the Eternal Return that growth requires. Every time you lose a loved one, you can only deal with one thread at a time. Recall, for a moment, a significant loss in your life. Do you remember how this one loss turned out to be intertwined with other times? But when you take your life seriously enough to address that particular one thread before you, over time, you will gradually find that your one thread is linked to every single other. You find a tapestry of connection that can lead you to your deepest truth and gift. You begin to realize that this one life is connected to the lives around you in unimaginable ways. Life becomes more colorful and vibrant, your energy, more robust. Over time, you begin to suspect that what warms your heart most deeply is there with purpose. Your skills and talents can begin helping you express creatively what you've discovered.

Who you are, your voice, your journey, belongs not only to you, but is part of the fabric of all to whom you are linked. The compassion for yourself, your failures and breakthroughs, spills over into your compassionate gifts to others. You realize your truest, most beautiful legacy is the love you leave behind in concrete traces, that your life can become even more of a 'love letter' through how you live. Taking the trouble to write out your story for your children, grandchildren, or future generations unknown to you helps you come full-circle, well-accompanied into one another's hearts. Albert Einstein, one of the greatest minds of the last century, put it this way:

> Strange is our situation here upon earth. Each of us comes for a short visit, without knowing why, yet sometimes seeming to divine a purpose. From the standpoint of daily life, however, there is one thing we do know: that we are here for the sake of each other. Above all, for those upon whose smile and well-being our own happiness depends, and also for the

countless unknown Souls with whose fate we are connected by a bond of sympathy.

So, your homecoming connects you with Life in its endless forms. If you do not leave behind your "field notes" in whatever form pleases you, everyone loses. We need one another's wisdom expressed in beautiful forms. In fact, as I told one of my mentors, Elisabeth Kubler Ross, before she died, successful grieving requires a step beyond "acceptance." If you really want to come back to life after loss, find a concrete means of expressing your love and learning as your particular way of "paying forward" what you've received. This is what coming full-circle means. I discovered this to be the additional sixth step to Elizabeth's five-step model of grief recovery: denial > anger > bargaining > despair > acceptance > creative contribution.

Must your "labor of love" be drudgery? Quite the contrary! The best offerings are homemade simply, from your heart, with complete delight. One woman I know moved from abject poverty to unimaginable prosperity from an attitude of focused intention and playfulness. Now an ordained unity minister, Edwene Gaines shares her pearls of wisdom with many around the world:

> Your life means what you say it is. So make up fun stuff. What would be the most fun thing you could do with your life? There are people in your life who do not know who you are. But this does not mean you don't love them. Nor does it mean that you let them stop you from living out your divine purpose.

Recently, Edwene was told by physicians that she should prepare herself for imminent death due to a blood clot in her brain that was about to burst. She didn't like this story. Having done the Western check-ups and testing, she turned the situation over to Higher Wisdom and Source. Shortly thereafter, a group from her church who had been praying for her received the imagery that she should fly to Latin America to see a healer by the name of John. Figuring she had nothing to lose, although somewhat skeptical, she told me she went to see this man. The result was that when she returned, the doctors could not find the clot. I make no attempt to interpret, but simply share with you the facts. Her story was reported in the November 2010 edition of *O Magazine*. I can tell you this: I've met Edwene several times, she is 'all about' having an enjoyable time, no matter what.

Activity without awakening is shallow. Awakening without its concrete expression is stillbirth.

Cara Barker

Prescription

To make your 'one thing' fun, who would you like to attract into your life? What sorts of people and circumstances do you want to manifest? How would you be expressing your love? Your creative self?

What would your number one focus be just for fun? (BTW: you are not the only one left to answer the aforementioned questions! I'm right here, 'in the saddle,' challenged by them too, at nearly eighty years old!)

Remember, when we lose our way to our heart, we lose our Wisdom, and future generations lose our love. Says Eldridge: "We don't need more facts, and we certainly don't need more things to do. We need Life, and we've been looking for it ever since we lost Paradise."

Keep the main thing the main thing.

Michael Clouse

Coming Home Exercise

What aspects of your story have been too painful to face? Too scary? Can you identify times when you felt overwhelmed or anxious?

_____

_____

_____

_____

Which old habits got in your way during these times?

_____

_____

_____

_____

What is the one main self-limiting belief that sabotages you today?

_____

_____

_____

_____

Which new habits do you need to acquire better self-compassion?

_____

_____

_____

_____

What one action step must you take to "come home" to the life you want?

_____

_____

_____

_____

How might trusting yourself to take this step begin a shift in your thinking?

_____

_____

_____

_____

What are you discovering? Which patches are most vibrant today?

_____

_____

_____

_____

SECTION TWO

Laying the Second Cornerstone: Your Foundation

"I want to give up all 'whys' and follow the thread that fascinates and delights the heart."

Meister Eckhart

CHAPTER 17

True Action

Remember the story I shared about those construction workers? Recall the challenges they had at first in demolishing old
previous homes before digging down into the earth to lay a sturdy
foundation for what was to come? It required lots of sweat and
mopping of brows in extremely hot weather. One worker told me it
was his "blood, sweat, and tears" job "requiring a shit-load of muscle
and bottles of water." And before it all, they had to make sure that
they were digging in the right place.

In these times of personal and planetary challenge, there's sort of
a cosmic flu going on around the planet that is showing up in our
lives as transition. Despite the many forms of unrest, you KNOW
that there's more to life than what the news reports. No matter how
good or how bad conditions are, people like yourself are committed
to living a better life. If that weren't true, you wouldn't be with me
right now. You would not be exploring how to experience more life
renewal, more joy, meaning, love, and well-being. You want to be
free. You don't want to miss any more of the things that really matter
to you. You know full well that living in ways that stress you out only
ends up taking you away from that 'truth that sets you free.' This is the
point of our time together. Every spiritual prescription and practice
that I offer here is for everyday life. Practice them consistently. They
will set you free to reveal the incredible human being that you were

designed to be in practical ways. If you are like most people, you will not practice them every day, and that's okay. But, as it is often said: "No guts, no glory." Just saying!

Not infrequently, I am asked what kind of freedom clients seek. They search for the best choices and actions they can take to be at deeper peace. Just this morning, at the French bakery down the street, a lovely Persian woman asked me the above question. So, I asked her the same question. She mentioned that she has felt dry, and at 51, she felt like she'd been in a desert. Her solution: entering law school at the University of Washington. She begins this month. Her daughter, on the other hand, cannot understand, since her mother had had much success before retiring. But I understand the why. She wants more life in her life. For her, this means discovering new things and continuing her learning. Her young daughters cannot fathom why their mama is choosing to do this. The fact is that maturing aids our relationship with natural knowing. Know this: I do not mean just getting older. It seems that aging without curiosity creates a penchant for discovery that produces crankiness, dryness, depression.

My new friend at the bakery is not alone. So many who come to me for in-depth psychology say something similar, especially if they are middle-aged or older. Once in a while, a younger person comes, but they usually carry a heavy backpack of trauma. Regardless of chronological age, each client wants to come alive again. More often than I can count, seekers come for life expansion, refreshment, and deeper meaning. Not infrequently, they describe stale relationships, feeling lost, living someone else's script and voice, and issues with love or their career. In every case, they have been misled. Consequently, this cornerstone requires re-evaluation. Not fun.

Rerouting our steps to more meaningful and enjoyable living gets down to honesty. A review of what's working in your life and what's not must be made. There are no shortcuts. I hate that there are no shortcuts! But that's the way it is. So, where do you start?

CHAPTER 18

Conducting a Life Audit

Whenever life dead ends, it's time to look in the mirror. Almost always, the culprit is that we have been following others' ideas rather than leading by our own intuition. Even when the 'previous life' has been rewarding, every so often there comes a time of stripping away what drains the Spirit, and exhausts body and Soul. Remember Jung's acorn metaphor? There is a mighty awakening wanting to happen in you and me, just as it is in that tiny acorn. Whenever you catch yourself feeling bone weary, it's *definitely* time to take action. What action? *Only* that which you notice *renews* your body, heart, and Soul. Remember this: just as the acorn has a mighty oak within, urging its growth, so, too, does our own Soul want original powerful expression in the now. What's the best tool that can be used to accomplish this?

Living a heart-led life can only happen with personal honesty. Whatever costume or mask you have previously worn in the world grows tawdry, threadbare, tight, for some, even suffocating. Needing to please others, be accepted, get applause, whatever, has run its course. It's time for your private audit.

Were you willing to begin and take a peek at this past week, or even month? Where and when were you left drained? For me, it was too many deadlines, taxes, and paperwork (I just hate paperwork!). When did boredom replace what used to be fulfilling? When and where did you want to vacate the premises? This is scary stuff. It is no small wonder that when we come to the edge of what was, our knees start shaking.

Backtracking is the norm. Here's a current example: a woman we'll call Lydia loses her husband of fifty years. Before he got sick, Lydia decided to retire. Being a realtor had served her well and had been satisfying at the time, which lasted over thirty years. But, as she put it, "I feel burnt to a crisp like overcooked bacon. I just hate Monday morning meetings. Always there is an urging for us to produce more, more, more."

Realizing how burned out she'd become, Lydia's answer seemed to be leaving the workplace. Lydia wanted to reclaim her days, minus any to-do lists. Two weeks into her plan, her husband, Henry, was diagnosed with lung cancer that had metastasized throughout his body. Within three months, Henry died. After handling death certificates, life insurance, social security, and the reading of Henry's will, Lydia described herself as 'spent.'

After profound loss comes loneliness, regret, and emptiness. Who wants this? Hence, we return to old structures, careers, activities, and often our historical 'go tos' when distressed (the internet, etc.). We know our old roles, even if they are no longer life-giving. One month after her husband's death, Lydia returned to her old real estate company hoping that "keeping busy" would solve how she felt. It didn't.

Psychologically, Jung calls this "regression of the persona." We knew who we were and our role before our loss. The problem is, moving backward delays crossing the edge to a new life. And this, my friend, gets in the way of laying a firm foundation for what our unique life needs to unfurl.

The profound ending of who we believed we were creates loneliness and interior frozenness. The challenge of meeting what has been is to come to terms with the fact of loss. This is part of its natural cycle if life is to become meaningful. No wonder most run away from the reality. If we can stand the pain, this is exactly where Soul fire returns.

Just this afternoon, a client from the past called me and said, "I've been so depressed. Finally, I realized that I've been grieving the loss of how I was before these two strokes. Once I 'got' this, my grief vanished. But first, I had to dig down to the bottom of this grief to find out the cause and my solution."

As my mother used to say, "We can't sit like a lump on a log and expect change."

Lydia faced the truth of her experience. She persisted in noticing when and where she felt most alive, most fulfilled, and most inventive. What limiting belief was in her way of taking the action steps she needed to take?

By way of an illustration: a forty-two-year-old woman named Donna dreamed she was wearing her mother's shoes. They were too big, too clunky, and too old. This client's process involved reevaluating where and how she was living in a way that wasn't Soul nourishing for her. What would fit better? She wanted a divorce, but her mother's beliefs that "divorce will ruin your kids, and why do you get to do what you want when nobody else gets to?" interfered with her progress.

Here's another mid-life client's dream. Sarah was struggling with feeling impoverished. Her mother was fond of advising: "It's just as easy to marry a rich man as a poor one!" Six years earlier, she had followed her mother's adage and married a multimillionaire. The problem was that the client felt trapped in an unhappy marriage and lost her natural joy. This is an archetypal story. Whatever must be cleared away is essential to finding new ground.

I am compelled to insert the following: at first, when studying Jungian theory, I hadn't a clue as to why fairytales and myths were relevant to our lives, and mine in particular. What I learned through my own interior dig was that a previously-unknown archetype was rising from the unconscious and playing havoc.

Unknowingly, we each are strongly influenced by our predominant archetypes. One way to find ours is to ask the question: what is my favorite fairytale and/or myth? When we locate it, we will notice its influence in the life we have built, to which we've been completely unaware. Over time and arduous work, I learned to love fairytales and what they reveal at a deeper level about the pattern of how we have lived, and what we've concluded.

For the woman who married the multimillionaire, I suggested to her to dive into the fairy tale called "The Red Shoes." Although she was unfamiliar with the story, when she did so, and later came to her session, she literally flushed when relating how important the story was for her. Let's review the tale.

CHAPTER 19

Archetypal Stories as Hidden Influencers

"The Red Shoes" introduces us to a young girl living in the forest, happily making her own shoes. She's a nature girl. This little one loved those shoes. But one day, a shiny, enticing carriage came her way, a vehicle owned by an old cranky lady. The beauty of that shiny carriage drew the natural child into it. Giving in to the temptation to live with the wealthy woman, tragedy struck. Trying to take a shortcut never works for our Soul. Hence, the young girl took a shortcut, and the end result was that she ended up losing both feet. Meaning, when reaching for the new 'shiny thing,' we lose our own natural way in the world.

It's not unusual that when our Soul, our Original Self, is in famine, we seek relief. There are endless forms of things that can temporarily provide that relief, too often the shiny things. When we stray from what is heart-nourishing, it is easy to get seduced by drugs, alcohol, gambling, videos, shopping, gossiping, overeating, beautiful carriages, affairs, or whatever promises to bring relief. Anything to fill the hole of lack. The danger comes from the fear of 'living out loud' on such a rocky, uneven foundation. Moving on demands facing previously hidden truths.

Now, I don't know about you, but when I discover that chasing the next shiny thing has led to a hot mess, I become aware that shortcuts don't satisfy. Shortcuts create bigger problems. Suddenly, we realize that superficial choices and shortcuts bring heartbreaking, unexpected problems and dead-ends. The naked truth is that something's got to give. As my mother was fond of saying in Finnish, freely translated: "It's time to get down to brass tacks." To take the necessary risks in life means big-time risk. No wonder we stall at the edge of taking a leap.

What is your Edge today?

_____

_____

_____

_____

What was your favorite story as a child?

_____

_____

_____

_____

One male client told me his favorite fairytale was Hansel and Gretel. Particularly, the children's worry about finding their way back home got this man's attention. Over deep work, the aforementioned client discovered that he'd been forgetting to notice the symbolic breadcrumbs; that is, hints, dreams, body symptoms, and synchronicities trying to help him.

CHAPTER 20

Facing What's Scary

With risk comes fear. A mistake that many of us make is mis-identifying what fear is. Remember saying or hearing, "I am afraid?" No, no, no. Just as we have a body, we are *not* our body. Just as we have thoughts, but are not our thoughts, so it is true with fear. Instead of telling ourselves the story, "I am afraid," how about instead telling ourselves, "I am in relationship with fear."

We must stop identifying with fear as if it were the whole truth. How? Let's use one of our most amazing attributes: our creative imagination. Each and every one of us are creatives. Okay, so you may tell yourself, "I can't draw a straight line." Nonsense! The afore-mentioned limited belief is just that. Limited.

Look around you. There's not a single thing around you that did not first come as a creative urge. I mean it: look around you. Someone you know or most likely who is a stranger 'dreamt up' that beautiful quilt, or curtains, or recovered lounging chair, or redefined how to tell time by going digital.

How did the end result of whatever surrounds you come into being? Simply this: somebody was brave enough to step through that portal which reveals new possibilities. Creative imagination counters fear. From that courageous step has birthed whatever is around you this very minute.

For weeks I've been telling myself I need to add tiny, shiny stars on a painting I'd been nursing. Ego mind countered by insisting, "Don't spend time on that. First, you'd have to go to Michael's and gather some materials. You don't have time. It's not that important. Forget it." Then, yesterday, I happened to drive by the above en route to another errand. Swinging around, I went into the store and marched straight to the materials needed. When I got home, I removed the silver stars from their bags. Slowly, I placed a few stars onto the top right corner of the image. It was so satisfying. Can I tell you why? Only that following the silent whisperings of your body or Soul, not your ego, opens life up in some mysterious way.

What's been itching inside you to create or construct?

_____

_____

What do you believe has been in the way of getting started on doing it?

_____

_____

CHAPTER 21

Employing Your Own Creative Possibilities

Here's one process that fires up creative imagination for the purpose of discovery. Jung called it 'active imagination,' by which dreams may be interpreted to bring rightful action. Say you have a dream or belly ache. What can you do to improve both a limited perspective as well as redirect the worn-out path you've been traveling?

Step #1: Check out whatever you've got before you, like a dream, symptom, or inspiration.

Step #2: Employ your imagination to bring dimension. Simply pretend you can imagine the shape, texture, smell, sound, and taste of this fear, and doodle its portrait. Get it outside of you, as if it were a character or cartoon.

Step #3: Close your eyes, take four deep breaths: inhale to the count of four, hold to four, exhale to the count of four.

Step #4: Pretend your subject has come for a conversation. Ask it: "Why are you here today?" Listen with your imagination for the answer. Ask: "What do you need to teach me? What's the root of my fear halting me from digging deep? What inside my thinking is blocking my progress?"

Finding the underlying cause of our present fear means taking action; getting 'some skin in the game.' We are talking about some deep digging. Uncovering the root/origin of what has been holding you back brings awareness of some previously-unrealized original wound. What is not excavated cannot bring liberation. Without it, we are left in the dark without a lantern.

For example, when I write, there's this little voice whispering: 'Is this really any good? Does this hit the mark?' That little beastie goes back to fourth grade with Mrs. West's red pen all over my paper. That teacher blasted me with, "Those are only sentences, not paragraphs." As I'd never had red ink on any schoolwork, a complex was born called 'I cannot write.' Clearly, this was not what she was saying. But it took a lot of shucking this old belief to release the pen from a hardened shell of self-doubt seeded many years ago. See what I mean?

One more thing. Some fears leave us frozen. But there are others that should be seen as valid warnings. For example, ever since I suffered from my aforementioned broken bones, now when I step down from a curb, I am extra careful and slow, so as not to repeat the injury. Body symptoms always, always, always are messengers to help us course correct however needed. So, too, are dreams.

Noticing

Most folks don't take either symptoms or dreams seriously as a source of interior guidance. Unfortunately, this leaves us in a muddle. Today, let's follow a more productive path.

Living a more nourishing life opens the road to what is deeply satisfying and nourishing to growth. Even the acorn needs to be in the right environment to grow. We need the right conditions to advance growth. Steppingstones are needed and simply must be in place if we are to engage in life with greater gratitude. With whom? It all begins by paying attention. To what? First, and foremost, noticing our own heart urgings as well as those of others along our path.

Who has inspired you to express more of your true nature?

_____

_____

Credit must be given where credit is due. You and I stand on the shoulders of those who have gone before us, leaving creative record of what it's meant to be human, despite distressing circumstances.

Hence, I am especially thankful to those Master Teachers who've modeled wholeheartedness, regardless of what the masses might have done, even when they have been given horrific challenges. Coming from diverse backgrounds and experiences, their lives and work are their testimony; a priceless contribution. Here are just a few: Frida Kahlo, Georgia O'Keeffe, Carl Jung, Emma Curtis Hopkins, Thomas Troward, Ernest Holmes, Emmet Fox, the great mystics Meister Eckhart, Hildegaard of Bingen, and our beloved national poets: Maya Angelou and young Amanda Gorman. Who has inspired you?

_____

_____

They needn't be so-called rock stars, or even famous. The barista at Starbucks was one of mine today. Despite an ever-growing line of customers, Kyle noticed an elderly woman with a black cane trying to navigate the heavy door. Off he went, with a, "Hang on folks. We need to help." He guided her to an available table while holding the bundle she was carrying.

Once she was seated, he asked the frail elder, "What would you most like to order? What would help on this freezing December morning?"

She smiled slightly and responded with a simple request: a small cup of coffee. "On it," this twenty-something young man replied.

Leaving her table, Kyle went behind the counter and busily prepared some surprise. Meanwhile, the little old lady struggled with her shabby purse, finally bringing out a black, worn out leather coin purse to pay. "No, no," said Kyle. "This is a gift from me. My grandmother lives on the East Coast and had to use canes. It's hard for her to get around these days on her walker, but I am many miles away. Not many notice her, and it breaks my heart."

Kyle was not asking for applause. He simply wanted to connect and make a difference.

You know, there is hardcore scientific evidence that kindness goes farther than we might think. Not only is the recipient touched; so, too, is the giver. Here's the surprising finding: those who witness humane acts are affected in positive ways, as well! (Healthy improvements have been measured, such as pulse rate and blood pressure. The opposite is true, as well, when marinating in an atmosphere of toxicity.) So, note to self: pay attention. Who is needing? Who is helping? Who is witnessing?

Historical accounts of surprising acts of kindness abound. Which of them has inspired you? In my case, I am left in awe by two men who did not know one another. Both were prisoners of war and terrorism. Neither allowed himself to indulge in defeat. When each were freed, their spirits intact, despite terrible conditions, Ellie Weisel and Viktor Frankl left an account of what it means to live wholeheartedly. Recall, each were hostages in Nazi death camps. Despite how horribly they were treated, neither gave up. Instead of succumbing to defeat, Ellie and Viktor accepted deep suffering and began to explore how they might serve others. Since then, what each has written and spoken has changed and enriched many lives, including my own.

How miraculous! I hate to admit it, but I'm afraid I would have indulged in a dark pity party in such dire circumstances. Not them. Each has had the courage to leave traces of their love in concrete form. We are the benefactors of the solid foundation they laid. The point is that whatever our experience, the way we respond to it scatters seeds. You and I will not know who's watching or what sort of fruit will develop from our seeds. Will the seeds turn out to rot or will they nourish? It's our choice.

Let's pause to review today. Let's ask ourselves: did we make a difference? Did we offer kindness? Have we expressed gratitude for life? Have we gotten better at self-care and self-compassion?

If you want to enrich your life, take only those
action steps based upon your Personal Truth.
Let authenticity be a cornerstone.
Let the rest go.
It will bring you to a great secret that
lives in your heart,
and shines in the world.

Cara Barker

Later, we will practice five things that can help you shift your relationship to living your Truth. If followed, you will most likely be amazed at what unfolds in your life. One highly successful woman told me that these tools and this process have given her "The License to Become." Don't you love it?

CHAPTER 23

Getting Our License

Here's a more local story from Maureen, who came to me to work on how she could lay a better foundation to live a heart-led life through identifying what her unconscious wanted her to know through spontaneous painting. Maureen, was sixty-four at the time. She'd been extraordinarily successful in the outer world for years. But apparently, she needed a means of accessing a deeper dimension of herself so that she could freely express her True nature without the fear that this would lead to too many consequences and interfere with getting the results she wanted, including paying bills. She wanted greater inner confidence, joy, and ease, no matter where she was.

Like her, you, and I, too, want to feel greater aliveness, to enjoy greater freedom, to spend your time doing more of what you want to do, and less of what you don't. You want to learn how to trust yourself more of the time, which means you want to grow. I know you see this creative urge in nature when you're paying attention. I love how Ernest Holmes puts it:

> ... there is a pattern of your being, or a real spirit of you, which is as Eternal as God, as indestructible as the Reality, and as changeless as Truth. This pattern is seeking to manifest through you. Back of it is all the will and purpose of the universe, all the irresistible laws of being. Finally, it will win.

Remember that old advertisement that goes: "It's not nice to fool Mother Nature?" Well, our nature insists that we are a recording instrument, a servant to our own heart's guidance, here, on this Earth, expressing our experience, our story, in the truest possible way, and this is the record the two of us leave those we love by how we live out the story we are creating today.

By way of a current example, I was just reminded of this principle by the following. It seems an American surgeon was deeply disturbed by the violent war between Israel and Palestine (particularly Hamas). Increasingly, via paying attention to his sinking heart with each news broadcast, he knew he needed to do something useful. So, closing his practice in America for a few weeks, he flew overseas to offer help to the wounded however he could.

Note that this surgeon did not look outside himself for what he might contribute. No, he validated his heart's Calling. How? By employing his skills and humanity where needed. Whatever our passion, this is our contribution; our way to serve. We are here as human instruments of love, regardless the form of our offering.

CHAPTER 24

Ethical Duty to Your Soul

I f the actions you are taking are conflicting with your true nature, trouble is up ahead. Count on it. Nature requires you to be you, and me to be me, regardless the price. If you want to "harvest more abundance," notice what you are doing that inhibits expressing what's truest in your heart. Where are you blocking your most natural Self from expressing Itself spontaneously?

How easy it would have been for the surgeon, described in the last chapter, to ignore his heart's urgings. How easy it would have been to talk himself out of going to such a dangerous part of the world amidst war. But he didn't. He answered the Call from his heart. He had no guarantees. Yes, he might have been killed or taken as a hostage by Hamas. He went anyway.

Dr. Jung called this our ethical duty to our Soul. Sound good? Then, let me ask you: are you ready? A truly fine woman by the name of Cynthia James reminded me recently of an old spiritual that I learned years ago, that goes like this:

Are you ready for a miracle?
Are you ready for a miracle?
Are you ready for a miracle?
Spirit will set you free.

Are you ready? Are you ready?
Are you ready for a miracle?

The problem is, as Cynthia and I have found, that we look for the miraculous where it does not live, outside ourselves. Know what I mean? We try to find the perfect relationship, or the perfect job, or perfect health, wealth, home, or community as if these experiences existed out there. No wonder we grasp for shortcuts. There are no shortcuts. We tell ourselves that what's wrong with our relationships is our partner, and we divorce, or what's wrong with our career is our boss, or where we work, so we look elsewhere, or that our weight or health can't be helped because we have certain genes, or inadequate inheritance, or an unfriendly community. We tell ourselves what we don't like in our lives is because of someone else. We are attached to focusing on lack. We focus on problems. The answer to whatever your problem seems to be is never focusing on the problem. Albert Einstein said it plainly: The answer to your problem is never inside the problem.

CHAPTER 25

What's Your Answer?

So, the answer to whatever your issue is today lies in how you've been framing the problem; that is, how you've been defining it. This propels us into false action. Which leads to getting in our own way. It's no small wonder that rates of depression, anxiety, and suicide have skyrocketed.

How to Turn Your Situation Around

Ask a new question. Consider focusing on your solution by returning to 'square one.'

Ask yourself what it would mean to live your most deeply-desired life. What if you claimed this intention? What if, at dawn, you said to yourself, "Yes, I AM ready for amazing miracles in my life today!"

Record your truthful answer here. What would it mean for me to live majestically, joyfully, and whole-heartedly?

_____

_____

_____

_____

Others would observe me:

_____

_____

_____

_____

Let me give you an example. A few years ago, we put one of our homes on the market. Everyone said, "Don't do it now. The market is terrible. You'll have to wait a long time. It's a mistake."

These people were not ready for a miracle. Well, we didn't listen. We put it on the market. Within thirty-six hours we had an offer. In less than a week we signed the papers. We were ready for a miracle.

Doing so is not playing 'let's pretend.' In fact, in the last decade, science has proven the relationship between our thoughts and results. This is not magical thinking. If you are ready, really, truly ready for more life in your life, if you are ready to get real about what is in your heart and let go, you must release negative thinking. Explore and practice mindfulness. Dump self-critical thinking. What others might call unbelievable, that's their business, not ours. Every single day I notice demonstrations of what's possible, regardless negative thoughts. What some call impossible, others experience with new joy.

I'm telling you this stuff works. Several paragraphs ago, I shared our experience of selling our farmhouse in what realtors called a 'disastrous' market. Our experiences defied common sense. Truthfully, the same unexpected breakthrough has happened for Ed and me a number of times during our forty-four-year marriage. (The only problem has been what my husband calls "buying high, selling low." Ugh!)

Prescription

Take only those action steps in harmony with actions that are based on the truth of your heart. Let this be one of your foremost cherished cornerstones, leading you home to personal authenticity.

So, what will it take for you to get ready? I'll tell you. One thing, pure and simple. The key is in your heart, your deepest desire. Take one little harmonious step, without hesitation, each and every time your Truth comes to you. Trust yourself more. Doubt yourself less. Take a stand based on what is true for you. Prepare the atmosphere to act only on truth by cultivating the skill to listen silently to your heart.

Meditate and take quiet walks. Learn to get better at becoming still. Here's where inner direction lives. You ready yourself for miracles by befriending stillness, by befriending that essence of what makes YOU unique, buried beneath too much self-doubt that is keeping you stuck. It takes time and practice to awaken the gift that you are. First, you and I must choose what kind of life for which we long to live. And what I mean by that is even more than seeking joy, we yearn for more aliveness in our life.

CHAPTER 26

You Choose:
Confusion or Clarity

Isn't it ironic that before we can take truth-based action, we each must practice skill-building to quiet our ever-busy minds? Otherwise, the noise distracts us until we don't know what step to take. *Confusion messes up clarity.* A cluttered mind produces an ineffectual life, leading us further and further away from what most deeply satisfies the Spirit and calms frayed nerves.

The fact is that you are magnificent. Yes, I repeat, you are an instrument of Creative Intelligence's divine expression. Now, you probably don't feel so divine much of the time! You likely doubt your beauty, your wisdom, your love, your direction, and your abundance, for this is part of our human predicament. You forget. I forget. We forget. This is why the world is in a state of such disturbing chaos and violence.

But just because you/we forget this, our true nature, doesn't mean that more is not possible. Not just the 'more' of acquisition. Frankly, the 'stuff' of possessions is just the training wheels for the curriculum of the real 'more.'

This is another subject for another time. Abundance in any form has to do with leaning into our experience, discovering our own Truth, and acting upon it by learning to follow the thread to our own heart's delight without the need to question, doubt, or diminish. There is a Truth inside you that carries the capacity to set you Free (with a capital 'F") in remarkable ways.

Your journey begins with an acknowledgement that when you lack this feeling of abundant aliveness and freedom, you must trust that this feeling suggests you are being inauthentic. Ouch. I know. But this is actually helpful to realize because it can be turned around in a way that's favorable to you. See, every single time you doubt it is possible for you to build a better life, self-trust falters.

Every time you hesitate to take action based on truth, your confidence and sound direction wanes. As recovering addicts put it, "You fall off the wagon." We get off track. I've witnessed this professionally in the lives of thousands of people for over fifty-four years. In books I've written, I give specific examples of those who, despite their noble intentions, have gotten a little lost. All of us experience these desert periods if we are honest. Not to worry though. Returning home to your own best self brings you through desert periods to the next oasis that awaits.

I know because I've seen this reflection in the mirror, although I would never have admitted this to you, or anyone, some time ago. We teach what we need to learn. I can tell you that shifting this human pattern does not happen overnight, unfortunately.

Let me paint you a portrait of how things can go down. As a second born of parents who came from immigrant families, I grew up trying to be a very obedient little girl, doing the chores that were set for me to do. The drill in my family had to do with getting a good education, becoming a responsible little citizen, accumulating many achievements, taking the 'straight arrow' path, staying in my head, and veering away from my deepest feelings. The good news was that this strict discipline taught me a whole lot about responsibility and hard work and opened many doors. The not-so-good news is that my interpretation of the game rules ended up literally masking over who I was at the deepest level. Finally, the estrangement and loneliness that comes when you try to negotiate life from an inauthentic place will just become too painful. Eventually the authentic you makes a break for it, no matter how old you are or how long your folks have been dead. Mine came in fits and starts.

Whenever you make your life too small, the psyche becomes turbulent. Up until then, your instincts sense that something is off, something is not quite right. That's how a highly successful woman described it to me a few days ago when she came for a consultation, as many well-known men and women have privately shared. Children, too.

Prescription

As you look back, describe a time in your life when you were living too small:

_____

_____

CHAPTER 27

A Self Portrait to Illustrate

As a child, I pestered my parents mercilessly as to whether I was not really adopted, which I wasn't. When I was a kid, something seemed off. What took many years and a lot of time, energy, and money to realize was that the sense of being an orphan was coming from a deep, internal knowing that it was I who was orphaning my most authentic nature. Many, many of us do this exact same thing. Hence, a large number of the cross-culturally enduring stories revolve around this theme. Now I know this, but back then, well, like most people, I was clueless. On January 28, 1946, when I was born at Walter Reed Hospital, I hadn't a clue how I'd come to this place, or how to survive this thing called 'life,' to which I was completely unfamiliar.

Looking back on those orphan musings, there was a pattern of organizing around distress in ways which created falseness. This showed up as a certain embellishment on much of what I did, as if who I was not enough.

For examples, my book reports were longer than they needed to be. Projects escalated into works well beyond what my teachers required. Enough just didn't seem to be enough. Let me illustrate with a few examples so you can see how these things manifest in our lives and begin assuming a life of their own, for which we pay a hefty price.

In junior high, my mother made me a polished blue cotton dress for a festival when I was crowned a 'May Princess,' based on the fact that my nine years in ballet, up to that point, brought me good posture. But when I saw the other girls' dresses, mine looked woefully plain. In secret, I stayed after school in Home Economics class to make streamers and a waistband for the dress, which I adorned with pearls and sequins. I slaved over my creation, believing my mother would never know. As I was escorted to the stage, there, in the very first row, sat my mother with her friend Sally Rowlands. Busted. My mother was so hurt that she didn't speak to me for three days. I felt not "good enough," and my mother felt not "good enough." My mother and I, it turned out, came from a long line of women who suffered the wound of "not-enough-ness."

When you slip into feelings of not good enough you are telling yourself a lie.

Cara Barker

We "shrinks'" call this state of inner turmoil "cognitive dissonance," which, freely translated, means that you've got warring sides going off in your head from two beliefs that seem equally true, yet are opposites. On the one hand, I felt liberated when I gave myself permission to create something original by my own hands. On the other, doing so resulted in hurting someone else . . . a conflict that stayed with me for ages. How do you create, how do you bring to life your desire, without harming someone else?

Trying to be who you aren't never pays good dividends.

Cara Barker

A recent example came from an attorney named Phil who frequently works out next to me in the gym. Phil is Mr. Success in the world but told me that he feels vaguely 'stressed out' much of the time. He put it this way:

> I've papered over the parts of myself I've sacrificed, but sooner or later, they begin seeping through the edges of the wallpaper and I'm left to deal with it.

At last report, Phil's blood pressure was climbing through the roof despite the fact that his body is what they call 'lean and mean.' I rarely see him when his jaws aren't clenched. The truth is, he's been mighty mean to himself, fixating on perfection rather than authenticity. He's forgotten how to play; a prerequisite for authenticity.

Sarah Lawrence-Lightfoot, quoted earlier, in her marvelous book, *The Third Chapter: Passion, Risk, an Adventure (in the 25 Years After 50)*, gives us hints. She has interviewed people who have become more transparent in the way they live their lives in their golden years and shares stories of people who have learned to navigate this conflict.

Listen in to Grace's story:

> She needs the silent structure, and reflective space of her studio in order to remain sane. But she needs the social contacts, the messiness, the discourse, and the energy from others to stay alive. Opposites need reconciliation to bring forward new life.

How has this sort of conflict borne out in your life?

_____

_____

_____

CHAPTER 28

The Good News About Conflict

The good news, as Jung points out, is that if we wake up to our conflict from dreams, body symptoms, and meaningful coincidences, and do good spadework, bringing awareness to bodily tension, something healing, something that expands our rightful place in the world by living authentically, opens up. His words were a welcome gift to me some thirty-five years ago and could be as well for you today if you are willing to face your area of tension squarely.

So, I began to notice that what I'd believed were archenemies within myself were actually trying to bring me a gift. Yet gifts need to be unwrapped, don't they? My own unpacking taught me that I had put my creative life on hold. I had begun to think of painting, writing, and singing as hobbies, not the main event. Up until that realization, my clinical work and creative life were at odds, kept apart from one another. I'd always loved the way people would tell me the stories of their lives, but never for one moment considered that my own illustrated saga could be something that would enrich my children and their children's children's lives as well as my own.

You see, as women, especially, we tend only to create something if it is for someone we love. I'm not saying this is a good thing, I'm only saying it tends to be so. This is why so many women eat very little after their family moves on. Creating a meal for yourself solo does not have the same punch or promise as creating something nourishing for those you love.

Earlier, in my junior high story, the adornments for my dress helped me feel like I belonged. On the other hand, they disconnected me from my mother. Whatever issue about authenticity you don't resolve will only show up later in another form . . . perhaps to give another opportunity to wake up. The Truth is necessary to evolve.

My own tale continued to unfold in an untruthful way until I 'got the picture' sometime later. Let me explain. Four years later, as a senior in high school, I embellished again. The art editor of our high school yearbook, one of my co-editors, pointed out to a few of us girls that there was a way of "doctoring up" the photos so that it appeared that our hair was longer and fuller. As I envied the curls of Georganne Rhodes and Mary Jane Scott (believing this brought them the "pick of the litter'" in the boyfriend department), I went along with the pack of other girls who were also caught in envy as we 'inked' in our photographs' hair to make it look better. When the yearbook came out, I was "busted" again. Nobody said anything until forty years later at the high school reunion. Two of my classmates shared with me how obvious it was that I had retouched my picture. Yes, I could see that my cover-up was a botched job. But, to have it pointed out? I was mortified. Trying to be who you aren't never pays good dividends.

Eventually, inauthentic steps led me to a nursing career that wasn't the best fit, because I thought it would please my parents. This false action led me away from a more authentic path in psychology in service to self-expression. The truth is that I had been interested in psychology. However, when I expressed this to our college coun-selor, Mrs. Forbes, she shook her head adamantly. "Oh no," said she firmly. "That track would not be nearly challenging enough for you intellectually. It would be a waste."

I believed the authority. Silly me. The prices I paid were huge. Living out others' expectations never satisfies. Something seemed "off." What I learned was that just because you are viewed as successful to the outer world, doesn't mean you are living your own truth. Although, I must admit that turning myself into a pretzel to please others helped me develop skillsets I otherwise would have overlooked. While I do not regret the past because of what I learned, the fact is that it is much, much more pleasurable now to live with greater ease in my system and without the strain of needing to be other than who I am to experience love. We can never get enough of what we really don't want.

Tell me I am not alone! What advice did you swallow from some authority that limited your life?

_____

_____

You can never get enough of what you really don't want to satisfy your soul's hunger!

Cara Barker

CHAPTER 29

The Road Less Traveled

W hen the pain became too great in my twenties, even I knew I needed to find my own "road less traveled," quite literally. The unconscious was sending prompts in the form of dreams of being in a death row prison cell for a crime I hadn't committed. And there was that repeating return of the aforementioned poem by Robert Frost, as I walked the Army grounds to the hospital where I was stationed. Heck, I didn't even understand poems at the time, but the meaning was not lost on me. I'd been walking the well-traveled collective road of false expectations and needed to shift my direction. Of course, this meant facing the consequences of disapproval. It also meant giving up my safety net and five year plan. I jumped, despite confusion, and life has never been the same. Tell the truth now. What's your 'road less traveled'?

Two roads diverged in a yellow wood,
And sorry I could not travel both
And be one traveler, long I stood
And looked down one as far as I could
To where it bent in the undergrowth;

Then took the other, as just as fair,
And having perhaps the better claim
Because it was grassy and wanted wear,
Though as for that the passing there
Had worn them really about the same,

And both that morning equally lay
In leaves no step had trodden black.
Oh, I marked the first for another day!
Yet knowing how way leads on to way
I doubted if I should ever come back.

I shall be telling this with a sigh
Somewhere ages and ages hence:
Two roads diverged in a wood, and I,
I took the one less traveled by,
And that has made all the difference.

Here's the irony. After a number of faux starts, I've ended up delivering numerous speeches on the subject of cultivating authenticity and how to really 'get real' about who you are. Since then, one of the most common pieces of feedback I've gotten, regardless of where I am in the world, is that I'm completely authentic. Sometimes things fly out of my mouth that aren't the best. But they are honest. This has been my Pearl of Great Price from battling my dragon of inauthenticity. In my book, "getting real" requires that we take Soul-directed action. Nature conspires, as Murray once wrote, to move us in the direction of the most unimaginable things to the moment you say "Yes." "Boldness," he said, "has genius, power and magic in it." So do you.

On those grey days when you doubt yourself, and both Murray and Frost fail to give you permission to be who you most naturally are, consider David Whyte's hard-won lesson:

You must learn one thing.
The world was made to be free in

Give up all the other worlds
except the one to which you belong.

CHAPTER 30

Down to Basics

So, let's get real with one another! Your story is not mine. Yet, each of us is responsible for living our best life, beginning with the excavation of everything in our lives that needs to go and then laying a new solid foundation. What might this mean?

I am fortunate because I know a few of the best construction workers to ask what is required when laying a firm foundation concretely, so we can use it as an analogy here.

Stress gets in the way of constructing the life we wish to have. I have learned something that has taken me years to comprehend. Hear the trumpets and drums? Here's the reveal: stress indicates taking false steps. Like me, the hundreds of thousands of people I've taught over decades have learned that your own stress-induced false steps only lead you further and further away from your own Beautiful Nature, your most natural Wisdom, and the most important thing, at the end of the day: love.

You deserve the best loving imaginable. Love is woven into your nature and is the most solid ground for building a heart-led life. Remember the song "Love is What Makes the World Go 'Round?" Expressing your gifts and talents in the most genuine way brings about a Greater Good for yourself as well as every single person with whom you interact. Besides which, becoming free to be who you are at the deepest level is a heck of a lot more fun than the school of 'fakin' it until you make it.' It's the best natural source of serotonin and anti-depression that I know of.

This, my friend, is not a concept. It is a Living Truth. You came here to be a magnificent expression of Life Substance, Itself. Sounds like 'woo woo,' doesn't it?

I don't care what you call it. Creative Intelligence does not make junk. You are here to live this One Life, this gift of the Divine, as the glorious gem that you are, hidden in the very ground needing excavation. That said, this is the time, and it's about time, for you to climb into boldness, speak your authentic truth, and join the parade, making an even bigger difference than ever before by living out what delights your heart. Long ago I heard Mother Teresa put it this way to her novitiates: "If you did not come here with joy and love in your heart, then you may as well pack your bag and go home. God is Love in action."

Since then, what I've learned is that neither you nor I can experience a Greater Good unless we are devoted to being that Greater Good ourselves. And by "good," I do *not* mean "goodie goodie," i.e., a phony. By "good," I mean that sort of honesty Mary Oliver describes in her marvelous poem that goes:

> You do not have to be good.
> You do not have to walk on your knees
> for a hundred miles through the desert repenting.
> You only have to let the soft animal of your body
> love what it loves.

This is your inheritance, and even if you doubt that such beauty is at your own core, you must find that small furry creature inside of you and practice loving this best part of yourself today! That's your job. That's your ONLY job. If you do this ONE THING, everything else will fall into place: your prosperity, your well-being, your self-confidence, your work in the world, and your relationships. This is TRUE ACTION. This is practicing the art of authenticity. Love the heck out of the one in hiding the only way that ever works: by being fully you, by moving in this direction. Notice that Oliver did not suggest you stay passive or idle.

Becoming authentic means you take your experience as it is and express the Spirit of Life without embellishment or charade. I know the Land of Razzle-Dazzle, of the add-ons and clip-ons, which have always gotten me into trouble. No wonder I was busted.

I'd gotten detached from my real value and believed I needed the extras to matter. But nature and the universe do not work through a lie. I was found out, and the price tag was shame, humiliation, and fear.

So, what keeps us from discovering that "soft animal" Oliver describes? Our hesitation comes from a distorted belief that who we are and what we experience is not going to win a popularity contest. Or, if you are a "cerebral" personality and believe popularity fails to motivate you, how about respect? Love? Do you ever fear that if you act only on your own truth that you'll be misunderstood, or, worse yet, ridiculed? Maybe you fear your experience is too pedestrian to interest anyone else. This is a lie you tell yourself to avoid taking a risk. I should know.

Nature does not work through a lie.

Cara Barker

The fact is, I finally came to realize that my own Way is 'the Way of the small.' Whereas my sister is a seven-course gourmet meal, I'm a "meat and potatoes" kind of gal when it comes to self-expression. You've just got to love kids because they tell the truth. When she was five, my daughter said to me one day: "Mommy, Aunt Linda is orchids, and you are daisies. We need daisies, too!"

Make life easier on yourself, my friend. Whatever your Way, it has purpose. Act on it, knowing this is your way!

Here are three basics that can empower you to build your strongest foundation by locating the beautiful hidden within your very Essence:

1. Make a break with those self-limiting beliefs holding you smaller than you are and interfering with creating a stable foundation.

There is an incredibly inspiring story about a prisoner-of-war named Bob Shoemaker, which I told in the audiobook entitled *Coming Home* (available on Audible in the future, time and wallet permitting), which has been widely recommended. Although he was tortured for seven years, Bob did not allow his thoughts to be captured by his wardens. Neither did Eduardo Garcia Valseca, whose story was aired on NBC in 2010. After his kidnapping in Mexico, Mr. Valseca was held for seven and a half months in a box barely wider than his shoulders. He was stripped and beaten daily, not allowed to talk, rarely fed, and had only a bucket for bodily waste that was rarely emptied. When Eduardo was released, he was suffering late stage severe starvation, three broken ribs, a damaged liver, and looked like a cadaver. What got him through this? Eduardo clung to what was real for him and acted on it. He told himself: "Calm your thoughts," maintaining focus on his wife, her banana pancakes, and the imagery of his children singing in a mariachi band. Despite the beatings and being shot twice by this EPR Marxist group, he survived not only his torture, but his self-torturing thoughts. Internally, he retained his most authentic freedom. He made truthful choices that were congruent with his Soul.

What about you? What story are you telling yourself that is holding you back from living your authentic truth? For example, I discovered one of my favorites was 'I don't have time.'

Identify one self-limiting belief that keeps you from being free. Record it here:

_____

_____

_____

2. God cannot operate in a lie. Neither must you.

If you want to have greater freedom, you've got to take action that assumes a greater good is on its way, already at work on your behalf. Even though this may sound too far-fetched for you, act "as if" this is so. Focus only on what matters to your best self and move in this direction. (Mine recently went like this: "I don't have enough time to paint in the morning, or review Spanish I took over fifty-eight years ago." Once identified, I saw the lie because doing the above means going to bed earlier and getting up at dawn. Case solved.)

God cannot operate in a lie.

Emma Curtis Hopkins

Your turn: Identify what matters most to your heart right now and record:

_____

_____

_____

Neither Eduardo nor Bob survived by telling themselves the lie that they were alone. They focused on what mattered to their hearts, connecting deeply with it, restoring a sense of honest purpose.

Identify what restores you and reconnects you with a larger way of living out the Truth that you are.

Author and physician David Hawkins describes this in detail in his mind-blowing book entitled *Power vs. Force*. Living in harmony with our highest Truth strengthens body, mind, and Spirit. Living in misalignment causes serious problems. Check it out. Study the lives of people like Viktor Frankl and Elle Weisel. Each of these men found interior freedom in Nazi concentration camps by connecting with their Truth, which involved discovering a greater meaning for their suffering and living it. Their willingness to dig deep inside brought forth their direction and showed them how to serve, even in these terrible camps. Nearly eighty years later, you have the same opportunity.

3. Cultivate gratitude for your present situation, no matter how your foundation feels at this moment.

Today, I am facing complete kneecap replacements, which cannot happen before four months pass. My choice is to complain or find a way through it. Once I decided to count each day closer to surgery, my stress vanished. Especially when I chose to name each completed knee with the name of empowered women. My replaced right knee I am naming Ruth Bader, the left, Frida Kahlo! I am grateful for my sense of humor.

Now it's your turn. Complete the following statement. I am most grateful for:

_____

_____

_____

This practice will get you through impossibly Dark Nights, and back into life and living. Six weeks after my only son was killed, he appeared to me in a dream, and gave me a lesson about how to deal with difficulties.

> Mama," he said, "life is a Schoolhouse. Everybody deals with something. The key to the Great Happiness is to receive whatever you're given, with complete Trust, taking Courageous Truthful Action, based on what you receive, even if you don't want it. Out of this offering comes Equanimity.

I've practiced this advice for the thirty-three years since his death. It is irrelevant to me if the story seems too 'woo woo.' It was my genuine experience. It has worked for me for decades.

If truth be told, I'll tell you that living gracefully and gratefully is not always easy. There are always bits and pieces of our experience that are tempting to censor. Not that you have to run around to the world at large and 'spill the beans' about everything. As Jung and others put it, there are some things that must always remain secret so as not to dissipate the gifts of the Sacred. On the other hand, your deepest, well-laid foundation guides you how to open and serve a Greater Good, to remember to cultivate gratitude, and get on with it. "Be gratitude" in every step you take. Even on crappy days.

One such example is my experience with the paranormal. Many times, people have shared with me their experiences with the mysterious aspects of life in almost a whisper. I've kept quiet about my own. What I mean by mysterious is those experiences that cannot be explained intellectually. Today, it is known that over 65 million Americans have had paranormal experiences, according to a leading expert by the name of Beth Wexler, a reputable social worker I met some years ago. Beth and I are well aware that even though many

many, many people in healthcare have had experiences of the super-natural, physicians aren't willing to talk about it, for the most part. Despite the fact that patients find these experiences overwhelmingly comforting and positive, I understand the silence.

What would people think? The blessing of being on the cusp of eighty is that it's much easier to throw off the shackles of these lies of omission of which I've been guilty, myself, and fess up to the fact that all my life I've had profound experiences with telepathy and clairvoyance. They have privately facilitated healing work that otherwise would have been impossible. The bottom line is that neither you nor I are alone. It doesn't matter whether you've experienced this hidden dimension of living, or, if you have a linear mind, you think this is garbage. Whatever your stance, let's get grateful. Where is your gratitude this minute? Mine is that you and I are together.

Significant help exists for you if you are willing to take a leap of faith. Those construction workers I described earlier are still digging to reach solid ground. Yes, they might find more gas or electrical lines, but they stay in the moment and trust the process. We've got to get that there is choice in all things. Even Jesus asked people whether they were ready to be healed. He did not plunge in uninvited.

This cornerstone gets down to one simple, but not easy, thing: it's your decision. Either you choose to live your life in the most grounded, stable way, or as if you were separate from life and the Greater Good. If you choose to act as if you were the Lone Ranger without his sidekick Tonto, you are living a lie. Authentic action requires that you make each choice before you in the direction of living out who you really are in a deeper, more meaningful way, giving yourself permission to enjoy the fruits of this practice. This is not done by pretending you are alone.

The operant word here is practice. If you choose to sign on for this adventure, expect slippage. After all, let's be honest: how many years have you slipped into the habit of believing that support for who you REALLY are is absent? Just like any sort of creative work, mastering the art of authenticity requires that you return many times to your life as it is this very minute. Consider yours a composition, perhaps like your life quilt. The way you think about this one life, of which you are a part, influences your next invention from it. Reinvent a more beautiful way to live today. How are you doing so far? You can do this! You came here to do this! It's all a matter of intention.

Where do you start?

In my group "Painting From the Unconscious" classes, I encourage students to "start from the angle closest to you." Where do you sense that you are denying yourself your fullest range of motion? Name it and claim it. That's your starting point. For example, for too many years, I denied myself the joy of reinventing how I wanted to live by waiting. I told myself stories like: "I can't create the sort of books, illustrations, and materials I'd like to until I have enough saved for retirement, or until the market improves." When you wait for guarantees, you are a living lie.

Prescription

Identify the joy you've been wanting to experience. For the next 48 hours, pretend you allowed yourself this experience.

_____

_____

CHAPTER 31

What Do You Want Most to Create Right Now?

One woman I know just called to tell me that she has just passed through her one year mark of sobriety: an amazing feat, indeed. Eighteen months ago, this powerhouse of a gal was busy creating all sorts of reasons why she'd never be able to sober up. She didn't, either, until she got real with herself about what was even more important and life-giving than alcohol: herself and her children.

You can do whatever you decide to do with practice, one day at a time, and sometimes one minute at a time. This *is* the applied art of authenticity: to create means to bring forward what has never existed in the same form before. This would be you. This would be now. This will require sincere coaxing on your part and a trust that you are not alone. Hafiz, a Sufi poet, expressed it long ago when he wrote the following. Let me share his gift with you, which he calls "We Should Talk about This Problem":

> There is a Beautiful Creature Living in a hole you have dug. So at night
>
> I set fruit and grains
>
> And little pots of wine and milk Beside your soft earthen mounds, And I often sing.

But still, my dear, You do not come out.

I have fallen in love with Someone Who hides inside you.

We should talk about this problem— Otherwise,

I will never leave you alone.

Who is this Someone that hides inside you?

This is the fully authentic you, genuinely expressing your Soul. Whatever is yours, it is integral to your foundation. Michelangelo's sculpture of David is analogous. This famous statue, which I saw many years ago at the Seattle World's Fair and again nearly four decades later in Florence, Italy, defies description. If you have not seen it, I can tell you that the figure is so real that you can easily imagine 'him' breathing. When asked how the Master was able to create such a piece of art, Michelangelo's answer was genuine: "I simply removed everything that wasn't David from the stone." (In our construction language, he cleared the land and went on his marble dig.) Michelangelo drew out what was hiding inside. This is your job, too. Okay, mine too.

Prescription

Do the following Practice beginning today, no matter how long it takes. Practice a bit each day.

Here are the basic instructions for your practice to remove and to shed everything that isn't your most authentic self:

For openers, check out your closet, junk drawer, garage, and wallet. Shed every single item that doesn't correspond to feeling fully alive, spacious, grateful, and current. Give it away. Sell it. Do whatever lightens the layers you no longer need! Do this practice for the next three weeks, getting rid of at least twelve things a day, and you will be amazed at the new life it brings you. Coax out the someone who's been hiding inside you just waiting for some space and permission. You have the right to release what is not conducive to being the best, most vibrant you. Stop thinking about cleaning out. Just do it. No guts, no glory! This does not mean that possessions are bad. It only means that if they own us, it messes up our foundation big-time.

Below, list the items you have in your closet, junk drawer, garage, wallet, and elsewhere which are leaving you too little space:

_____

_____

_____

_____

How is holding onto these objects getting in your way?

_____

_____

_____

_____

What story have you been telling yourself as a way to avoid cleaning them out?

_____

_____

_____

_____

What action steps would resolve this?

_____

_____

_____

_____

CHAPTER 32

Redrawing Your Blueprint

Not only can you rewrite your story, but you have the God-given right to revise any blueprint which holds you back from expressing your most authentic nature.

Your revised construction plan requires action. You can try to kid yourself that you'll think about your rewrite, but this is a sham. Writing, the kinesthetic movement of your fingers on a surface, has a power to it when combined with clear intention. So, don't kid yourself. As Welch poet David Whyte has put it so succinctly: The world was made for you to be free in.

Where are you feeling crowded, with less range of motion than your heart desires?

What did you describe in the last question in Chapter 31? (Or did you pretend the exercise was not for you? If so, go back. You are worth it.) Whatever your condition, give the way you see it a turn. For Georgia O'Keeffe, this meant telling herself the truth. In her words: "None of the paintings I'd made were for me! Every single one of them was to please someone else. . . . So, I took every one of my paintings down, and vowed to begin again, at first, in charcoal, until I'd drawn out the strange things in my head . . ." O'Keeffe decided to create what inspired her in new ways, doing so became medicinal. She empowered herself to create from her heart. In this way, she became an artistic medicine carrier.

Frida Kahlo made a similar choice after she was nearly killed in a streetcar accident. Her heart-led decision created a more meaningful, vibrant life. From that point on, she painted only *her experience*. This had never been done before in the art world. Each of these artists of life got real about their own personal experience and used their years of training to serve their own Truth. Doing so changed art history and gave license to millions of others to begin trusting their own process, by shifting their perspective. Hence they began constructing from a truer foundation. They 'rewrote' their stories using basic materials to which they felt drawn that caused delight.

We human beings are never happier than when we are expressing the deepest gifts that are truly us.

Os Guinness

Sometimes we just get stuck. A colleague and good friend of mine, Helen Luke, consulted her work partner, Robert Johnson (a Jungian Analyst), when she had no idea what her spontaneous painting was trying to tell her about being in a dilemma. Said Robert: "Helen, just give it a quarter turn." Literally, Helen turned the painting and immediately, she had her 'aha' moment about the revised direction of her life.

A Historical Metaphor to Help You

Like the historical figure David, O'Keefe and Kahlo had to confront their own Goliaths. Remember him? Goliath was the Philistine giant that David slew with a stone from his slingshot after the giant threatened the well-being of the people. Symbolically, you could say that Goliath represents our overwhelming thoughts and beliefs that hide our authentic nature: the nay-saying thoughts, perpetrated by the ego, which stir up fear and self-doubt. Like Helen, we tend to waffle when we should stand resolute on the ground of our own inner Truth. "Goliath thoughts" are the ones that menace and weaken you, diminishing your aliveness and enjoyment of life.

Prescription

Describe the "Goliath thoughts" which have limited you this past week:

_____

_____

_____

_____

Enter David. The origin of the name David means 'beloved'. Applied to you and me, this means we each are beloved and have a beautiful nature unconsciously, even if the two of you have barely met. Your "inner David" nature has to do with your inner Wisdom that restores harmony, feeling, awakening connection to the most sacred part of who you really are at your core. Your David nature awakens the Truth that you are intimately connected to an all-powerful life substance that informs and molds every living creature and all of nature in accord with whatever story we tell ourselves. Our "David aspect" ushers in a new way of constructing a better way of living.

CHAPTER 33

Transformational Medicine

In the Western world, the word medicine connotes an image of pills and injections. Historically, though, healing was thought expedited through herbs, plants, prayer, sand painting, dream groups, music, dance, and painting. In most parts of the world, these forms of medicine are still practiced. Doing so evokes happiness.

Cultivating the Art of Authenticity is good for your health! Blue Zone studies, done in areas where people exceed 100 years of age, are increasingly indicating that happy people, (people who feel free to live out their best lives), not only live longer, but also healthier lives. The happiest people do not believe their inner Goliath! They activate harmonious conditions for their life.

Dr. Gene Cohen, my friend who once headed the Department on Aging for the National Institute of Health, found important evidence that supports the findings of this latest research. When we express ourselves creatively, it has a harmonizing effect on aging. Gene once told me that: "It's never too late for us to become who we really are!" He was a powerful advocate of continuing to develop purpose by becoming mentors as elders.

Harvard researchers agree. Their findings are in concert with the latest developments in neuroscience, demonstrating that when you follow the course that most delights you, the brain conducts electrical impulses that shift the circuitry in a far more beneficial and powerfully creative way. This brings about tremendously engaging expressions. The question, you see, is not *what* have you been thinking, but, if you gave yourself the time and space to de-clutter your thoughts, and leave room for the Stillness. What new impressions, inventions, or creations that you've never thought before might enter your field of awareness if you did so? Give it a try. If same old, same old is draining you, what do you have to lose?

Harvard's Mind/Body Program has impressive documentation that when our serotonin uptake (the naturally occurring feel-good chemical in our body) is flowing, along with neuro-peptides and dopamine, this expands your neural pathways, meaning that it sets up a network system in the brain which promotes a greater sense of well-being, heightened creativity, and appreciation of creative collaboration. Not bad, huh?

How do you do this?

It's simple, and yet not so simple. You develop a regular practice. You commit to a process (for example: yoga, meditations, mindfulness, prayer, chants, etc) that speaks to your heart and strengthens your immune system function, lowers your cortisol (the body's stress chemical), and promotes a deeper experience of harmony, well-being, and creative connection and expression.

I have found that an infallible means of practice is to enter some form of Depth work. Recording dreams, expressing them creatively in some tangible form helps their symbolic guidance come to life. You need not be an artist, musician, dancer, or sculptor to do this. Even colorful doodling counts. Remember it is not words that nudge change as potently as creative imagination expressed in concrete form.

How? Let's begin. You must practice this for a minimum of forty days, no exceptions. Recall me mentioning that there is no overnight, express lane, or shortcut to what you want to create in your life? No devotion brings no results. Whatever practice you choose will work. It doesn't have to be religious, but it could be if you desire. Taking a walk in Mother Nature, unencumbered by phone or demands, becomes my personal sanctuary and inspires helpful, imaginal guidance (for more on this, refer to my third book, *Nightlight*).

No devotion nets no results. You deserve better.

Cara Barker

Believe me, I've heard all the "reasons" why practice is not possible, beginning with my own monkey mind chatter, and I have heard it, as well, from many international clients. All I can tell you is that if you are telling the truth about wanting a more liberated, inspired, peaceful, and exciting life, then you've got to be willing to give up the stories you tell yourself. If nothing changes, nothing changes.

Let's say as a kid you wanted to learn to ride a bike and develop mastery of that skill. Could you have mastered this skill by reading about riding a bike? No! You needed to get out there and practice every day. Once you got the rhythm and the coordination down, you were free to do some mighty great riding. The same thing applies here. According to Malcolm Gladwell in his book *Outliers*, the biggest 'greats' in the world in every arena have logged in a minimum of 10,000 hours in their own practice before they developed mastery. This is a big league commitment that bears big time results. Setting aside time daily to focus mindfully has been the single most important sacred practice of my life in terms of bringing enriching freedom, growth, and inspiration, because it reveals to yours truly the essence of my foundational cornerstone.

CHAPTER 34

Practicing Basic
Truth-Based Action

The following basic practice for strengthening your relationship with who you most naturally are involves securing time and space for an appointment with yourself. Although the process comes from the Harvard Mind/Body Institute, you have permission to record it for your private practice. Or you may prefer to use an upcoming meditation series that I will be offering in 2025 for a nominal fee (see carabarker.com for details). Likewise, by 2025 this book will be available as an Audible on Amazon.

True action comes from truthfully expressing your innermost, honest, heart-based experience. Committing to this true movement, stepping out into your world based on your innermost knowing, and nothing else, is the single biggest game changer for your life. No joke. Trust yourself. You have a secret world inside you; a secret, beautiful story that's waiting to be told through the way you creatively express who you really are. Practice this faithfully. Your life will open up in amazingly gratifying ways!

Prescription

For now, close your eyes. Become centered through deep breathing. Open yourself to receive what arises from your creative imagination.

Others on their journey are finding it helpful to record the following slowly and listen each time in their own voice.

1. First, imagine a beautiful scene. Stay with it, as if you've entered it completely.

2. Second, "hear" sounds through your creative imagination. Dwell here for a moment. Enjoy.

3. Third, allow words or a song to come to you. Relax. Write them down.

Revisit this through the day for thirty to sixty seconds and enjoy the process. Do this whenever you are feeling indecisive about something.

Whenever you feel tense, do a body scan, letting go of heaviness, stress, fatigue, and any issues that might be troubling you. Give yourself permission to lay down these burdens for now. Simply enjoy breathing in and breathing out.

Whenever you are feeling pushed, imagine yourself returning to that beautiful scene, sounds, words, or song that came to you. Trust their guidance. Let go. Act only after you have centered yourself this way.

1. Now, imagine yourself completely centered, relaxed, unburdened, moving toward your inner home. Return home. Come home to who you are beneath the layers, to your most beautiful creature. (We all have one. You, too.) Notice the shyness, giving yourself permission to take your time, breathing, relaxing. Leave room for imperfection. Leonard Cohen says: "Ring the bells that still will ring. Forget your perfect offering. The cracks are how the light gets in." Let some light in. Enjoy the cracks. Return once more to your creative imagination's beautiful scene, sounds, or words. Breathe. Center.

2. Now, move into a place of greatest beauty, calm, and harmony that is surrounded by a feeling of gentle kindness and opening. You are dwelling in the area that is your heart.

3. Using your creative imagination, invite an experience to come to you that would bring about the greatest joy, the biggest relief for you today.

4. Dwell in this experience, breathe it in deeply.

5. Notice some gentle little sensation that nudges you toward a tiny baby step in your life today, a little practice you'd enjoy for just a few brief minutes which would move you in the direction of becoming and enjoying your own self. Perhaps it is a few moments in nature, or making a little phone call, or writing a note. Perhaps, in the silence, you were given a little saying to write down and use throughout the day to maintain contact with this experience. Whatever comes is exactly right for you. The messier the better. Tidiness is a truth killer.

Breathe in your gratitude and breathe out all that distances you from gratitude.

Know that you are moving in the direction of greater well-being than ever before. Release all need to strive and drive yourself in directions that are not the real you. Imagine a beautiful scene, that helps you relax even more. Breathe. Imagine it with all your senses. Relax. Enjoy. Here's a space for your own notes:

_____

_____

_____

_____

In closing, listen to Annie Lamott's words:

> We begin to find and become ourselves when we notice how we are already found, already true, entirely wildly, messily, marvelously who were born to be . . . so the real issue is how do we stop being who we aren't? How, indeed! Practice, practice, practice!

CHAPTER 35

Traveling Beyond the Life
You've Been Living

You want to move forward. This means a leap of faith in how you perceive who you are in relationship to the world.

You need to learn how to make the jump between a literal perception of the world and a metaphorical, symbolic one. This is what I call "the Work." It is to teach that everything is a map. Everything.

Everything is a map. Everything.

Everything has to do with some sort of internal blueprint. It's not a question of discovering meaning where there is none, but rather a question of staying with those feelings and coming to important realizations about yourself, your strengths, about what you have to do in this condition of apparent meaninglessness. By now, you know what it's like for your circumstances to include something you neither planned nor wanted. You've known discouragement and difficult, unexplainable losses. Here, you must understand better how to love and how to work in your own way, no matter how small it may be. The lessons you must learn in facing trauma and disappointment have to do with acknowledging the preciousness of life and the importance of caring for yourself, not neglecting yourself.

What aids the healing is learning to be within the present experience while able to observe the Self in relationship to said experience and its implications. This necessitates a willingness on your part to move through the doors that are opening before you. You've kept them closed up to now. I say dwell in wonder every day!

For example, a man I know very well told me last night that for the first time in his life, he is beginning to wonder whether there might be life after death after all. Religion has never been his "cup of tea." Yet, following the death of his only son in a plane crash before the holidays last week, this father has experienced events completely foreign, and reassuring, about love and the Beyond. He is making room for a question mark, not because of what anyone has either said or done, but from comprehending that Presence in the moment. I understand. When my own son was killed, I was left to consider the implication of three dreams I had that showed me his literal death the year before it happened. After his death, the scene at the funeral was identical to one of my dreams. There were various electrical phenomenon following his death which I experienced in the company of others; too many to mention. Then, there was the dream I had following his demise that explained our relationship to the Divine, in which Matt's friend, Grant, was included. When I awoke, I wrote the dream down and shared it with my husband. The dream indicated a Greater Love at work through each of us. Two weeks later, Grant wrote to me. He'd had the exact same dream the very same night. Go figure! We do well to open our minds to the unknown. This means practicing being completely in your experience while witnessing it, versus splitting from it. This takes cultivating a strong and healthy sense of Self and getting grounded.

Your task is learning how to transcend the apparent form or appearance of things into a deeper level of understanding. We must learn to go beyond preconceived notions of how to express our experience and yield to new forms. Going through the afore-mentioned stories even shifted my way of parenting.

Traveling beyond where you've been challenges you to defy your pattern of hiding who you are. It's a way of challenging your inclination to conceal your Self, your fear, your pain, and your gifts. When we've been raised as children in homes which lacked the capacity to support our inner worlds (hiding our tears on the bathroom towel rack), we were forced to seek privacy to deal with our issues without knowing how to ask and receive help for such much-needed solitude. As children, we needed more opportunities to retreat into our inner world but lacked permission to do so. Eventually, it led to distancing ourselves from what was most needed for our very Soul. So, if you want to experience more freedom, notice when you interrupt yourself from being fully present.

Healing comes from mastering how to *simultaneously* enter your private inner world, while at the same time being available in the outer public way. It is a terrifying journey at times, and not for everyone. I remember well my hesitation in writing and sharing my own experiences. Today, this is no longer permitted. You and I are challenged to learn how to walk again with a foot in two worlds: the inner and the outer. Prepare to limp for as long as it takes. As for me, while waiting a few months for knee replacement, I am using a cane. Wherever we are limping, psychologically, spiritually, mentally, or physically, let's get going!

Your Third Cornerstone: Framing a Heart-Led Life

What can help us reframe the construction of a heart-led life?

Take Maggie, another client, for a good example of reframing the life you are building anew. There are going to be times when you, like Maggie, are frustrated, alone, and discouraged; times when you question pretty much everything and start to doubt yourself. You may have noticed that during these places in the labyrinth, you are lacking in self-compassion. Maggie described herself this way when we first met, after her doctor sent her to me following a rough diagnosis. Like you, she worked extremely hard to be happy; as she put it: "to think positively." This had been Maggie's way of framing how she should live. Maggie had a long history of sidestepping the disappointing things, and "putting on a happy face." She had been to an Erhard Seminars Training and was afraid that she had caused her terminal illness.

Since her seminar, she made many sacrifices to have a better life; as she put it: "to not be a victim." Maggie invested in what her head told her would bring joy. Even when she felt good, it never lasted long. Still, maybe like you, she did what my mother called 'plugging away.' She was a good little soldier. Eventually, she came to see me because she wanted to feel good more of the time, in the time she had left, and unhappy less of the time. She was also lonely and frightened. This state had nothing to do with 'being a victim,' but everything to do with her experience, which she was hiding from others.

The Value of Dreams

And so, I requested that she trust herself more and bring a written copy of her dreams. Margaret did as I asked. For quite some time, Maggie, as she liked to be called, brought bits and pieces of many of them, discounting her dreams' worth to help her. Eventually, through all her dismissal, a dream series took shape with a journey theme. Over and over, Maggie found herself searching for something missing. Sometimes she searched at the seashore, or mountains, along a riverbed, or through a forest. Now, I should add that right before she came for a consultation, she had experienced a life-threatening heart attack.

She was searching for what was missing from her life; from her heart. Her heart was under attack. What she didn't know, until this particular dream, was that It was searching for her. I capitalize 'It' because It was huge in every way to Maggie's Spirit. The 'It' is known by many names. Call It whatever you will: Soul, the Self, Creative Spirit, your greater Unlived Life, God, Buddha, the Akashic Field, Atman, Mary, Sophia, Kwan Yin, Guadalupe, or whatever. Regardless the naming, this is Universal Life Force, regardless Its costume, pushing to express love, wisdom, beauty, vitality, abundance, peace, and freedom through each one of us in concrete ways.

Maggie secretly wanted a more colorful, creative, connected life. Privately, she'd struggled for a long time with the habit of working too many hours with a deeply-seated desire to quilt. She longed to bring the pieces of her life together in a cohesive and colorful whole. But, before the heart attack which nearly killed her, she talked herself out of spending time with her heart's desire, rationalizing that doing so was irresponsible. Says who? When Maggie 'met' her more natural Self in that dream jungle described in Chapter One, the figure looking for her was holding an amazing quilt of many colors, portraying a woman on a journey.

A Big Dream for Us All: A Message for Our Times

Carl Jung, the famous Swiss psychiatrist who studied cross-cultural dreams, is known to have commented that there are small dreams, of the personal variety, and there are Big Dreams, which have importance to us all. Maggie's was one of the latter. She gave me permission to share it with you because its message includes you, and yours truly, getting more out of life. It is particularly crucial for your family and mine, given what is going on in the world.

What Maggie discovered was that she had never considered that, just as she was seeking the missing piece of her life, that she was being sought by the seeker. In her dream, an enormous and beautiful being she called the 'Great One' came to meet her across the river she'd been hesitating to cross. The Great One advised Maggie:

> Marvel more. Worry less. Everything is unfolding as it needs. Stop pushing yourself. Start trusting yourself. When you worry about the future, forget it. This is a lie that's bad for your health. You, and others in your world, have forgotten how to live freely. When your world forgets this, you disconnect from the Truth of how to live in harmony and peace with all Creation. This is

why your civilization is beginning to unravel, your structures breaking down, your governments unable to govern. People hating people they do not even know. Your people have forgotten we are all One, living in One Field. Your people have fallen asleep. Without a Higher Purpose in how you live, you will never come together in Sacred Way. Begin telling a new story through your lives. Life is impermanence. Best to be here, to enjoy the moment, to discover where it is leading, and to say 'yes.' All is well. This is the Way.

The Secret and the Sacred

Each of us has our own way of arriving, of traveling through this life stumbling over obstacles called fear. You have heard the statement: "The Truth shall set you free." John 8:32

You don't have to be spiritual or religious for this to strike a chord, do you? Something in us resonates to it, isn't that true? The question, however, is which Truth? Where is it located? How do you find yours? How do you take back your life and live it as joyfully, as passionately as the child who marvels, dancing through the spouting water feature outside Starbucks on a hot August morning? How do you awaken from the stupor of indifference?

All I can tell you is that there is a mighty Force alive in you; a Force whispering to you regarding what you need to reframe about yourself, your purpose here, and your life, as surely as it was in Maggie before she died. There is a Mighty Force alive in your affairs, in the green- and red-throated hummingbird flying over my purple petunias today in my garden. This Mighty Force reminds me that I am not my circumstances or conditions, not my experiences, nor fears, nor thoughts. Every one of us are more than this. It is this Force that is ever-faithful in It is seeking you, guiding you to greater love, self-compassion, self-permission, and to an experience of wisdom, beauty, abundance, vitality, and freedom to the degree to which you let It guide you, to the degree you allow It to live through you, to the degree you are willing to lay down the burden you've been carrying in favor of opening to the more you came to be, do, and have right here, and right now. Let me assure you:

Long after your mother and father, and all you have known is gone, the Spirit of Life remains. That which seeks you will still be here. Let yourself be sought. Enjoy the dance. Trust your process. This will bring you Home to the much, much more that waits in the secret hiding place where your best self lives in your heart. A million times the small mind says, 'why bother?' Don't listen. For that which seeks the Spirit of your life will go on to call your name even more times. Advance in the direction of your heart's desire. Trust that your instincts will not fail, Its Truth will set you free, bringing you rest if you give yourself permission. Fan the flames of your Spirit to dance again in the name of something greater than you've ever known; for something greater than your ego's self-created identity. And how does the seeker guide us so well? It guides us to the secret truths, where it lay hidden in the cave of our heart, the cornerstones and steppingstones of our foundation that support a peaceful heart and Soul.

Let your light shine. Let your life become your best love project that you were sent to be. Bottom line, each of us are put on this earth with one mission. Very simply, we are here to serve something beyond our own ego.

CHAPTER 36

Acts of Recognition

Remember the house Juan and his crew were preparing for the next stage of building a beautiful dwelling? He told me that "if the foundation was messed up, it would mess up the framing."

Accurate framing, whether it be a building a house or building a more heart-led life, is crucial to what will stand the test of time. This includes the studs and laths fastened accurately so that these timbers can best support the floor and ceiling. Every single step deserves full attention.

Believing you are not enough really gets down to the fact that enough of you has not been expressed.

Cara Barker

Put all that you are on the line in celebration of the life you've been given. Begin this practice: create vehicles that express your truth. By this I mean you will know that you are on the right track when your heart is lighter and your spirit lifted. Leave traces of your love as your footprints for those who come after. When this seems too tough, consider those who will follow you generations from now. Consider how helpful it would be for them to have traces of someone's journey back home to more love, beauty, wisdom, and what such a journey has meant.

Stop validating your self-critical voice. Bringing love, wisdom, and beauty through your voice in some concrete way becomes your Act of Recognition.

Regardless of the Act of Recognition you design, it is an important rite of passage. As the Gnostic Gospel of Saint Thomas puts it, ". . . if you bring forward what is within you, it will heal and save you. . . . If you do not bring forward what is within you, what is within you will destroy you."

Having accompanied many people during their dying and transition process, I can assure you what Saint Thomas said is true.

When you feel you are being told "you are not enough," this really means enough of you has not been given full-expression; has not been voiced.

Prescription

Lay yourself fully on the line. Imagine yourself at the starting gate, saying with all your might: "I stand, or fall, based on taking this position 100 percent."

You and I must run our own race. No one can fill in for you. You cannot live your true life by proxy. Your race does not gain merit by who you ran alongside.

Ultimately, you must do your work. I must do mine. Others must do theirs. That's how it is.

This is why the issue of creativity is so vital to living heart-led lives, regardless of whether or not we consider ourselves to be artistic in any way.

As an aside, a dear friend of mine, Artemis, just brought a feast from her Greek Orthodox church. She told me, "Everything in your home is pure beauty."

I told her that beauty is but one expression of the Light because beauty brings harmony from chaos. "That's because you are an artist," she said.

"You express beauty through your generosity," I replied.

She laughed and said, "No, it's just easy for me to do these things. They give me joy."

Bingo. What Artemis said are the hallmarks of her gift, the very foundation which frames her life. Now she is off to support her friend leaving for Turkey but is having car trouble. See? Artemis to the rescue. What seeds of grace she leaves with her footprints.

Each of us must address the issue of our own creations. It is through the creative process that we achieve any form of immortality that at least survives us in form. And, by the way, each of us creates every single moment based on what we choose in the now. We must never dismiss or negate our contribution. The size of it does not matter.

What we leave behind are seeds, as surely as the oak tree leaves its acorns, we leave traces of our love for the gift of life, for the process of discovering our own heretofore hidden "beautiful creature," bringing it out into the world so it can breathe and be known, valued, and expressed.

As we accept the importance of this, we pay it forward. Most of the time, this is a truth of which we are unaware. Here's an example. When my son died, in his dorm room was the last paper called "The Real Me" that he wrote for his psychology course at the university. Honoring and recording his authentic nature was the greatest legacy he could have given.

Here is another example. In my parents' case, my mother recorded, at my request, her "Pearls of Wisdom" in her arthritic scrawl for her grandchildren, one of whom was not yet born and the other who would follow her in death nine years later. My father, on the other hand, left behind six recordings from when he was interviewed by the Eisenhower Museum six months before his sudden death. These are traces of love, which all are now among my most meaningful treasures. Priceless. When a door opens, it is on us to walk through, even though the results are none of our business.

Gift-leaving asks us to contact and translate the deepest part of our experience of having lived. When you lose your child, you must become your own legacy to the next generation. You no longer are left with the indulgence of placing the burden on the shoulders of your children or grandchildren. What it births is a part so deep in the darkness, in the shadows, that you did not know it was there before. But whether you have lost a child, or even have a child at all, none of us is "off the hook," as we say in American parlance.

Prescription

In the aforementioned, I gave you a few samples of Acts of Recognition that others created which outlived their creator. Whether you accept it or not, you are leaving traces of your original nature, which will become your legacy. The question is, are you and I leaving sufficient traces of love? As a officiant of some weddings and funerals, I've noticed that when these "rite of passage" events come to life, it is not until the original details of what the person loves and most deeply cherishes, that a light of this lost life force comes back into the room. All the rest is the blah blah blah, and not the Presence that touches our hearts.

Practice

These gifts are part of laying your framing cornerstone for your updated, heart-led life. If it were possible to put all of who you believe you are "on the line," this very minute, as a voice of celebration for a heartfelt gift of life, what form would be the most enjoyable for you? What would be fun or inspiring or meaningful for you to include in your own Act of Recognition for Life? For me at this very moment, it is writing this sentence to you. Now, it's your turn: take a leap of faith and record whatever comes from your heart without editing what you write:

_____

_____

_____

_____

_____

Use your journal or blank pages at the end of this book to draft ideas that come to you which touch your heart. Fill the page and then get your "rear in gear." We just never know. Before my son was killed, he wanted us to author a book together. I promised him we would. Nine months later, when he was killed, the pen was left in my hand. Although writing was the furthest thing from my mind when I was growing up, now it is a full-time companion. You just never know.

Prescription

This is your space for all "add-ons" that come to you later. Be sure to include the date, including the year. Over time, if you are patient, you will discover an exciting, life-renewing theme. (In Jungian work, we refer to this lifelong theme of passion as "the red thread."

Unfortunately, we do not know ours until much further down the road, as we get much older. The retrospectraocope is advantageous.)

For example, over thirty years ago, when I began writing and recording, and over forty-five years ago, when I began making art again, I had no idea these avenues would merge into one theme which would eventually evolve into the chief aim of my life direction. Nor did I realize that these simple works would become my legacy to those I would leave behind whenever my "walking papers" would come.

Much too often, too many people get distracted by intellectually striving to find life purpose. I know I did for years. The answer to such a question can only be found within. The only way to develop a heart-led life is to shift our focus from the outer to within. To find it, we, too, metaphorically must come at night and set out fruit and grains, and little pots of wine and milk, and often sing "to that Beautiful Creature living in a hole you have dug." As poet Mary Olver said. Such a courtship will take the rest of your life if you are to know the supreme joy of living a heartful life which can only set you free, leading you home to that Love pouring through you, despite mental obstacles, building heart-led living, based on the firmest foundational cornerstones.

CHAPTER 37

Dealing with Contradictions as You Move Forward

Journeying back home to your best self so that you can leave traces of your love involves facing contradictions. But the question is: how do you live with inner contradictions? For example, in relationships, the mixed feeling of "I love you and hate you at the same time." Or, how can you be incredibly sad, yet at the same time, a part of you feels a rejoicing at the edge of a certain form of enlightenment? How do you deal with guilt for the part of you that rejoices even in a time of tragedy? No doubt you've experienced things like gallows humor, as if we're getting something out of the tragedy. We need to stay with the contradictory elements that exist in every profound life situation. Truth is always paradoxical; it's never black and white.

Framing well a more meaningful way of living, which is coming home to that beautiful creature Hafiz describes so delightfully, requires a certain grieving as you travel beyond the life you have previously known. Our grieving is for us: the death of our identity and life as we've known it. We are left to reinvent our identity. We must face our disempowered parts and release these ways of concealing parts of ourselves out of fear. Your task, and mine, eventually, is to dare to be vulnerable; moving through your accepted public image (the husk of who you are) of trying to be "somebody" or nobody.

I'm talking about being fully alive and finally free. There's a tre-mendous opportunity in our journey, including loss of the familiar, to discover our own natural life. But part of our framing cornerstone requires that we let go of the little boxes we have kept ourselves in.

This is your chance to get skilled at befriending yourself. The required cornerstones cannot be laid without learning to be kinder and more encouraging to who you are meant to become. Think of this mysterious road as a superb opportunity to develop self-compas-sion, which means relinquishing your stress and strain from trying so hard to be who you aren't.

I've told you how such a futile attempt thwarted me in my own life. Thankfully, I'm not alone. The question is: what about you? What contradictions have caused your struggles? My friend, contradictions are a bugger, especially when it comes to solid framing.

As a little illustration, mine was centered around the conflict of how to create what delights me most without hurting someone I love. What might be yours? Don't worry about finding the perfect words or answer. Trust what comes. Begin your draft. Your understanding will deepen over time. Fill in the following: My conflict has centered around the contradictions between . . .

_____

_____

_____

_____

Again, let's recall how Albert Einstein put it this way:

Strange is our situation here upon earth. Each of us comes for a short visit, without knowing why, yet sometimes seeming to divine a purpose. From the standpoint of daily life, however, there is one thing we do know: that we are here for the sake of each other. Above all, for those upon whose smile and well-being our own happiness depends, and also for the countless unknown Souls with whose fate we are connected by a bond of sympathy . . . .

Now to arrive at this place Einstein describes, you've got to make more room for your "cracks," imperfections, and flaws. You've got to laugh more at your quirks and stop taking yourself so darn seriously. No matter how long you live, life is too short to live in a perpetual state of the description I invented called terminal 'seriousity.' Yes, the world may call you a fool or think you've "lost your marbles." Who cares? The fact is that life is strange. You can make it a melodrama as most people do, or you can travel into what's coming with a sense of amusement and dance when least expected. It's your call.

All I know for certain is you must stop abandoning what you need most. You must stop abandoning your heart's desire. You must reclaim what lifts and nourishes your Spirit most, especially when you notice that you have vacated the "driver's seat" of your own life. Likewise, you must stop abandoning yourself when the road gets bumpy. We Westerners suffer from the belief that life should always be easy. Growth stretches us. When you were born, what if your mother gave up because labor was too taxing?

Welcome difficulty. Learn the alchemy. True Human Beings know: The moment you accept What troubles You've been given The door opens . . . .

Rumi

.... the last of the human freedoms, to choose one's own way.

Viktor Frankl

You came to this Earth through birth contractions, and this is our lot if we are to advance in the direction of our dreams. Rumi had it right when he said to "welcome difficulty."

Prescription

During your "short visit" here on our Earth, describe the most meaningful gift of service you could offer:

_____

_____

_____

_____

Describe the difficulty you must learn to welcome:

_____

_____

_____

_____

What doors would you love to open?

_____

_____

_____

_____

Remember what Confucius advised us?

Wheresoever you go, go with all your heart.

Confucius

Bulb Woman Original painting (in color) by Cara Barker, 1991

Whatever beautiful creature lives inside you, remember it comes from a very deep and hidden place below the surface of your life. Cultivate a relationship with your depths, for therein lies the source of your greatest secret joy. Be not afraid. The dark and mysterious are the soil of your own most natural being and foundational to heart-led living.

CHAPTER 38

The Audacity of Connection

When it comes to framing the best heart-led living, we must keep our feet on the ground and pay attention to the living. Now, these days there is an ongoing conversation about the importance of connection to our well-being. Yesterday, while waiting my turn at the bank because my credit card was hacked (yes, again), I noticed four other folks sitting there, as well. All of them had climbed into their smartphones. A fifth entered the waiting area. He had white air pods lodged into his ears while looking at his screen. I began to remember the days before our 'connection' devices. Back then, the norm was to establish a conversation, if only a hello. (Even today, in Zurich, if we do not welcome a passer-by with a cordial 'guertzi,' we are considered rude.) Connection used to be available. Today? Not so much.

If we have no peace it is because we have forgotten we belong to one another.

Mother Teresa

There is a well-known wisdom from the Delphic Oracle that goes "Know Thyself." What isn't said is equally important. How can you know yourself without a loving connection with who you really are? Who you really are beneath the layers of fear, self-doubt, and self- criticism is nothing but loveable. I have this on good authority! What it takes to get to this place is self-compassion. A sense of humor doesn't hurt, either! Listen to Einstein once more. His words merit memorization. Forgetting his message brings only more strife and mess. If we do not frame our daily action around knowing who we truly are, then the life we are building will not be an improvement, but instead more 'the same old, same old' like the house that will soon become a 'tear down.' Einstein observes:

> Strange is our situation here upon earth. Each of us comes for a short visit, without knowing why, yet sometimes seeming to divine a purpose. From the standpoint of daily life, however, there is one thing we do know: that we are here for the sake of each other. Above all, for those upon whose smile and well-being our own happiness depends, and also for the countless unknown Souls with whose fate we are connected by a bond of sympathy . . . .

Our task is discovering and mastering interbeing. This bond of sympathy begins with having compassion and tender regard for your 'good enough' self. This world is too tough without it. Too isolated. You get derailed when you dismiss your right to connect with your deepest self, and others. Every time we 'check out,' like the folks in my bank's lobby, we miss the important things. As an illustration, while my lobby neighbors had climbed into their devices, they missed what I saw outside the window. A little girl in a blue seersucker sundress with gleaming blond curls crouched down on the sidewalk to hug a beagle puppy. In harmony with the little one's expression of love, the puppy was busy licking her rosy cheeks.

It is on the threshold that sacrifices to the guardian divinities are offered. . . . The threshold, the door, shows the solution of continuity in space immediately and concretely; hence their great religious importance, for they are symbols and at the same time vehicles of passage from the one space to the other.

Mircea Eliade

It is on this threshold of preoccupation, especially today with all preoccupation with devices that blocks the magic of the moment, that leaves the life we are framing off-kilter. A friend of mine, and fellow writer for the *Huffington Post*, Kari Henley, shared with me a story about a young girl in her area who was raped. Here are Kari's words:

> In the town next to ours (a very upper middle-class town) eight fourteen-year-old boys took turns sexually abusing a young girl on New Year's Eve in a basement while the adults were upstairs partying. . . . the issues of bullying and guns are almost a constant dialogue for children in elementary school through high school.

The really sad thing is that this story is becoming increasingly common, as are other acts of bullying, which, at the extreme, become terrorism. These situations begin with self-disregard.

One of my favorite sentiments of Carl Jung's was, "Where there is love, there is no need for power. Where there is power, there is no love." In continuing his work over the years, I'm clear that Jung wasn't saying that it is wrong to express who you are powerfully, with confidence. He was referring to the fact that when your intention is one of deep and abiding connection for greater good, then grasping for the power way only brings out the worst in yourself, your community, and your government.

The fact is that, as pointed out earlier, we live in inner states of contradiction. No wonder stories like those of Mary Magdelene and Martha draw attention from the New Testament. While Mary was at the feet of her teacher, Jesus, her sister, Martha, was in the kitchen acting like a victim. (I imagine her banging pots and pans.)

These stories symbolize the parts of us at war that we project onto others, like the bullies in the basement who harmed the innocent girl as the parents upstairs were oblivious to what was going on in the basement.

We forget we are related to one another, that we are related to One Life. We forget to relate and embrace the parts of our own hearts that have been abandoned. The opposite of love is not hate. It is indifference. We must give up our indifference to one another, and to the Wisdom of our own hearts. Without this, no attempt at building a better life will be supported.

Emptiness is always here. It is the emptiness in the cup that makes the cup valuable, because into the emptiness we can put our tea or coffee. It is the empty space in the room that allows us to move around all things. Come out of emptiness. Form and Emptiness are two sides of this Mystery of existence itself.

Marianne Williamson

Consider this: our hands must be empty to receive goodness. In these times of broken-heartedness, when powerful opposing forces at play, we must step out of the fray. Let there be space for something valuable to settle. Looking at the events in today's news, you might be asking, "But isn't it impractical, unreasonable, and even adolescent to believe in framing our evolving life in Love?" You might be saying to yourself that this is horse caca. I would understand. Because In the midst of daily scenarios of bullying, teen suicide, terrorist plots, and scams, what kind of a nutcase must you be to believe that such a thing is possible?

And yet, all the teachings and practices of every major religion have championed the Imperative of Love. Let's take a look at a few:

Taoism: "Regard your neighbor's gain as your own gain and regard your neighbor's loss as your own loss."

Judaism: "Thou shalt love thy neighbor as thyself."

Christianity: "Love your neighbor as yourself."

Buddhism: "In five ways should a clansman minister to his friends and familiars—by generosity, courtesy, and benevolence, by treating them as he treats himself, and by being as good as his word."

Sounds like love to me! "But wait,'" as the late-night info-mercials put it, "there's more!"

Sikhism: "As thou deemest thyself so deem others. Then shalt thou become a partner in heaven." (Okay, a little wordy, I grant you, but you get the drift of the same message. Freely translated, how I frame myself, I project onto others.)

Hinduism: "Men gifted with intelligence should always treat others as they themselves wish to be treated."

And not to be overlooked, **Islam:** "No one of you is a believer until he loves for his brother, what he loves for himself."

The Golden Rule is a universal one. But, from our own experience, you and I know that just because something is a universal teaching does NOT mean that it is a universal practice! Our predicament, as Cain and Abel demonstrated, is that we are "split-apart." We want to love, yet we fear loving and being loved. Apparently, what our Spirit knows as Truth, our little monkey minds have a difficult time trusting, much less practicing. Instead, we turn our focus to judgments and whining. Emma Curtis Hopkins, one of the great Master Teachers from the nineteenth and twentieth centuries got it right when she told her students:

> Complaining and whining are only exhibitions of the great desert spots in your character. You must fill up deserts with rain and fertilizer. So, you must transform your moments of complaining by praise. . . . The desert has not enough rain, so you have not clarity and mercy enough if you feel like complaining.

We'll come back to the importance of the love desert, and how it affects framing a better life in a bit. For now, suffice it to say that if you've observed yourself having a whine-fest lately, you're actually bullying yourself. I can tell you that you are living in a way that's drying up your Spirit. This is dangerous business; the business of the desert. Let me explain.

For three years I lived in the Arizona desert. One of the first lessons you learn in places like that is to always carry more water than you need. It's been said that if you get stranded out there for only an hour, you will die. I became a believer. In fact, this whole period of time became my stint in what's often called your "forty days in the desert."

Ever hear of the forty days in the desert? This metaphor comes up repeatedly in the stories of spiritual teachers. Jesus had his forty days in the wilderness; Buddha, his forty days beneath the Bodhi tree; and Moses, his forty years in the desert with complainers and whiners. The number forty is symbolic, because it has to do with wholeness. When you travel through a desert, either literally or psychologically, you are attempting to come back into alignment with yourself via what you endure during this uninhabitable dry spell. "Who cares?" I know! But this has to do with you, if you want to be free to create a better life.

You want more love in your life, right? Sure, you've got your things to do today, you've got your list. But, tonight, as you lay your head down on the pillow, what's most important all gets down to love. Doesn't it? And I don't mean love that equals obligation. I'm not talking about that sort of clichéd Valentine's Day stuff which reduces most men, in the Western world, to a state of distress for fear of the sense of obligation and the press of expectations. No, by the word 'love' I mean that experience which reconnects you with your heart at the core level, connects you with an experience of belonging to a greater good, connects you to finding joy in the present moment.

Here's an example from yours truly. As I was pondering the clock, in order to resume editing what you are reading, a stream of sunlight flooded my living room. Although the clock was ticking, the beauty outside seduced me. Out I went. Thinking I would only take five minutes, I sat down on our rocking loveseat. Three seagulls flew by, drifting with the breeze. Time, I am sure, was not directing their flight. Beneath them, Lake Washington was aglow with golden light, so much so that the waves sparkled like diamonds. Paddleboarders slowly and gently used their oars to move in the direction the wind was calling. How easy to notice that my black flowerpots were overflowing with bright red geraniums and purple petunias. Meanwhile, to my north, the seven-foot rose bush was unveiling dark pink rosebuds, as if being called to fully blossom. When I looked at my watch, forty-five minutes had passed. I do not regret one minute. Nature, including plant life, water, sky, birds, and paddleboard people regaled me with the riches of slowing down. It was the best dessert I could have ordered!

Think back to such a time, no matter how brief it may have been. Recall the feeling of this sense of true connectivity with something indefinable, yet nourishing, healing, and uplifting. Regardless the condition of your life at that moment, recall that "all is well, and all manner of things is well" experience that just makes you feel good to be alive, no matter what the circumstances or consequences. Describe what you recall. Fill it in without censorship.

I remember:

_____

_____

_____

_____

These memories are paradise moments, aren't they? When they happen, suddenly, you and I are transported back to possibilities. Elizabeth Barrett Browning captured it with her advice to "dwell in possibilities!" Indeed.

If you think about it, everything you've ever experienced, everything that's affected you most deeply, has had to do with either being infused by this love, in the presence of a greater undefinable good, or else it has had to do with the desert experience of estrangement from this good. Unfortunately, the journey of building a better inner home foundational to this experience of loving yourself in the very real world requires a journey through the desert. And what is the impetus to missing the gold? Running and pushing ourselves . . . for what? Isn't it annoying? I hate this truth. The fact is, however, that every single developmental leap means slowing down and, yes, the tougher experiences when we pushed and pushed and missed the moment we will never get back.

The question is: how can Love flourish in your driest times? How is it possible to continue practicing, operating out of faith, when your life hits zones of misery? Sure, it's easy to feel good when things are going well. But what about the times we prefer not to talk about, much less have them in our life story? What about those epochs when the well has gone dry?

By way of illustration, I assure you that I've have my own chapters in this desert story. I've asked these same questions. I've attended others asking them of me wherever I travel to do this work. It's easy, but not comfortable, to recall one such time.

Around thirty-plus years ago, I was down. I was dry. Much of what I'd dreamed for my life, you could say, was pretty much "burnt to a crisp." My son had been killed eighteen months earlier. I felt like one of those people on Oprah Winfrey's show that I'd overheard a few years earlier, each of whom had lost their child. I recall thinking at the time how horrible this would be. No, their chapter was not for me! The day the news came to my own door, it was surreal, as it is for every bereaved parent, I assure you. It takes a long, long time to take in the enormity of what's happened to your whole picture of your life, love, and your relationship to a greater good. Most perish in the process.

Well, like I said, I didn't want this chapter in my life. Life said, "Tough. This is what you've got. Deal with it!"

Five months later, my husband's career necessitated a move to Arizona, which meant that I had to start from ground zero to build a private practice and leave one that was already flourishing. The move would mean feeling cut off from the friends I had made while I had been living in Washington, D.C. I was in the desert, all right. Zoom was still far into the future.

Here's the ringer: this literal and figurative move and surrender to the desert led me Home to a fuller, more honest relationship with life. Not that this means I'm saying that losing my son was worth it. No, let me be clear. All I am saying is that we get what we get. Sometimes you love what you get. Sometimes you hate what you get. The Universe doesn't care. You get what you get, and your job is to discover how you are going to respond in the truest, most life-renewing way, or you're done for. You get to choose. Do you roll over and play dead, or do you choose to grow forward from your challenging circumstances? Rumi suggests it's best to have passion for whatever you've got than to ". . . be a dead fish in the ocean of God."

Well, back at the ranch, one thing was clear for me. I was hurting. I knew it. I knew that this sense of arriving at what seemed to be a God-forsaken place where I did not want to be at all, caught in living a life which was dryer than dry, placed in a spot where people seemed to be on a completely different page psycho-spiritually, economically, and politically was most definitely not my idea of a good time. I was grieving, big-time. And I'm telling you all this as a means of prompting you to remember your own period in the desert, although your time there has its own unique details.

Frankly, despite my years in the trenches ministering to others, I was clueless as to what to do in this barren place. So, I did what I've always done: I turned it over. I meditated. I went on walks. I painted. I prayed but seemed to be getting no answers. Eventually, I spiraled down to the bottom of the well. I prayed. I waited and waited some more. I prayed some more. The pithy little church clichés people said annoyed the hell out of me just as much as people who tried to analyze the whole thing psychologically, or with their woo-woo sayings.

Eventually, in the heat of this angst and despair, I had a dream. I dreamt of a benevolent Wise Woman by the name of Sophia (symbolic for the Feminine Face of God), who told me I must follow the "Road of Roses," and there, I would find Her in the desert by the fountain of Living Waters. That morning, after I got my daughter to school, I hopped in the car, followed my nose, and ended up synchronistically at a place I'd never been on Rose Lane. Saint Maria Goretti's Church stood smack on that corner. Unable to resist, I went inside. There, I found the woman in the dream. I spent about an hour and a half sitting in front of her statue. And, for some inexplicable reason, I felt better. There seemed to be something so comforting, so compelling about the experience that I just sat there, breathing in and out what seemed a rarefied air.

Other experiences came too, as the deepest place inside myself responded as though I had come Home to what was truest for my heart. My heart was warmed, my Spirit lifted in such a way that I knew I was going to be alright. Eventually, I wandered outside and began to wonder about the water in my dream, and the Tabernacle also pictured in the dream. Beyond that side door, I stopped in my tracks. I was facing the dream Tabernacle, inside which was the exact same fountain, the Living Waters. I went inside, sat down, waited, and meditated. Sophia's voice from the dream came back to me in the stillness of my heart and said, "I want you to go to the women who are calling for their oasis. I want you to help them find their answer. I want you to show them the true meaning of an oasis in the desert: Our Answer Speaks in Sacred, Symbolic, Somatic Story: O.A.S.I.S."

Now, I ask you: what would you make of this message? I had no answer.

When I opened the front door to my home later that afternoon, the phone was ringing. My long-time friend, Linda Granat, a big-time event planner in Seattle, said, "I just felt I had to call you today. I've got some women who really want to work with you. They are feeling dry and need you to create an oasis. Will you come and lead a retreat?"

You can guess the answer. That request turned into a set of retreats that I conducted for the next nine years, until another dream, and another assignment in Asia. Love has an audacious way of leaving clues if you learn how to listen and take the time to hear, meaning we have to reframe how we live a heart-directed life. (By the way, if you are an engineering type of person, like one of my family members, you will shrug this off as fantasy. If so, I don't care. The experience was alive in me.)

Oh, one more thing. The day before I was to leave for Seattle to lead the retreat, I felt something completely new to me: a complete resistance to going. Suddenly, my Spirit was in the desert again. Although I'd never, ever canceled work with a group before, I knew I had to come into connectivity with what was in my heart. Again, the phone rang. It was Linda. "Is there anything I can do?" she asked.

I told her of my plight and begged off. "No problem," she said. "Let me think about it. Whatever you need is fine. Let me call you back."

What a trouper! I couldn't believe she wasn't angry, or even upset. Never mind that women were coming from different areas, their bags already packed, their tickets purchased. True to her word, she phoned back in about an hour. "I've been thinking about this. You are exhausted. Get on the plane. I'll pick you up. I know the kind of healthy food you love. I just called a great massage therapist. I'm going to take care of you and show you where I walk beside the water every morning. This time, it is your turn to be taken care of." I will never forget this gift of audacious loving. "You can spend the time meditating and just being quiet, whatever you need. My only question is, would you mind if I set up the same thing for the other women? You don't have to do a blessed thing for anyone. I just want you to feel better!"

True to her word, Linda did as she said she would. She picked me up at Sea-Tac Airport with a hamper of goodies, and had Ron Hogan, the masseuse, waiting. I've never been so cared for in such a generous way in my whole life. By the time the day ended, after the evening meal in silence, very organically, the women and I ended up by the fire in the living room. In the most natural way imaginable, the process began, and has lasted for many years as we began to come into full true relations with one another's hearts. There was not one thread of obligation in it, just an honest desire to come together and enjoy the experience. Living 'wholeheartedly' restores, rejoices, and reclarifies why you simply must find compassion for yourself before you can serve others.

What happened for me here renewed my life and shifted its course, which never would have happened without the desert. I learned much later that this place, Saint Maria Goretti's, has a history of recorded mystical experiences. Go figure. All I know for certain is that the love speaks through many languages, including the dream, synchronicities, and concrete structures with very real histories, even though we have no conscious awareness of them. Love leaves demonstrations. It lives in our intuition.

Sometimes, this Greater Good speaks locally, through people who express themselves naturally and without a manipulative agenda, because they know that the foundation upon framing a renewed life is love without condition or obligation. Sometimes love boldly speaks through the interconnectedness of things that cannot be denied. But, always, when Love demonstrates Itself, you feel better. Your Spirit feels renewed. Your faith is restored in your own process and in others. When it does, new little shoots of life spring up in your heart as evidence that you were never alone, even in the desert, where desert flowers do eventually bloom in red, pink, purple, and orange.

Prescription

Now, it's your turn. Remember that little practice I showed you a while back?

Remember using your creative imagination to return to a

particularly beautiful scene with sounds and words? Revisit this in your mind's eye. Relax. Now invite a memory of some unexpected experience where love showed up in an unusual way for you. Record it here, including the particular details:

_____

_____

_____

_____

A lovely twenty-something young mama asked me recently, "Why don't these things ever happen to me?"

I asked her for her explanation. "Maybe my life's too vanilla," she said. "Maybe I'm not open. But I'd like to be."

_____

_____

You see, my friend, and I'm talking from my heart to yours now, we know that we want more Love in our lives, don't we? You know there's more for you if you would just open your mind a little more, your heart a little more, a little more time each day.

The fact is that sometimes you have to lose your way to find your way back home. What's waiting changes everything. Enduring stories describe this phenomenon.

CHAPTER 39

A Legend of Audacious Loving, and Non-Local Love

I'm reminded of one such legend from the Middle Ages. A very loving young nun, by the name of Beatrix, was a devotee of the Virgin Mary. Each day in the convent, Beatrix took splendid tender care of Mary's shrine. As time passed, a priest seduced Beatrix, however, with his protestations of love, and talked her into leaving the convent. When she became pregnant, he abandoned her. For many years, Beatrix suffered shame and humiliation, but attended to raising her child with her whole heart, just as she had the shrine.

One day, after many years, she returned to the convent and asked whether anyone remembered a young nun who was called Beatrix, to which the woman who answered the door quickly responded, "Why yes, but, why do you ask? She is here and devotes herself to the Virgin Mary every day with great love and kindness!"

Naturally, Beatrix was shocked. Miraculously, that very moment, the Virgin Mary appeared to Beatrix and explained, "My dear, your love is clear. I have been here, in your place, until your return. Now you are free to come home, here with us, knowing that you are, and have always been, surrounded with love, without condition."

I love this story, for it mirrors my own experience. You and I might fall into seduction by those things which do not last. Maybe you've gotten seduced by false lovers, or perhaps by jobs that were not right for you. Perhaps you feel that you have made some bad choices about where you've lived or how you spent your money. Maybe you've gotten conned by someone who you supported. We might condemn ourselves for our stupidity, and yet, a greater Love persists, awaiting your return to the heart of who you truly are. It does so with neither judgment nor self-bullying.

So, if you've gone astray, and you refuse to forgive yourself, just be clear that it is not Love which holds you hostage, it's the bully in your basement, your unconscious, that has a field day raping your Spirit and torturing you with self-recriminations which have absolutely nothing whatsoever to do with either what is true or what is Love.

Beatrix's story points out that a Greater Good lives in you, and me, no matter what you may be facing. This Good awaits your devotion to serving whatever is your Greater Good, which can only be defined by your own heart.

Stop lamenting what is gone and start focusing on that which is decent in you and praiseworthy in your heart. Devote yourself to living with a more grateful heart. Jung called this the Self. Others call it the Soul, the stillness, the diamond, the Bodhisattva nature, the rose, the lotus, the pearl of great price, the Christ consciousness, the God within, and so on. Love wears many costumes and speaks whatever language you need it to speak in order to practice creating a more heart-led life. Trust me. Trust your heart. Trust what is beyond human understanding in that invisible realm beyond what we can measure. A greater love awaits your reunion with something beautiful: the real you.

Seek and ye shall find. Knock and the door shall be opened.

Matthew 7:7

Non-local Love

Something greater than Beatrix's idea of herself waited patiently for her, as surely as it does today for you. One of my experiences of this came when my son died, a year or so before we went to the desert. Some say angels are "out there" in the ether. However, what I discovered in grieving my particular loss was that the greater good is expressed through loving kindness in the form of friends, strangers, and other bereaved parents. My experience taught me that we are angels for one another whenever we are courageous enough to show love This is non-local Love, radiating through the local.

If you've ever seen the photographs taken by Dr. Emoto of water crystals that have been immersed in beakers on which individual words are taped, such as "love," "hate," "blessing," "war," and so on, you may recall that the crystal photographed with "love" and the one for "blessing" were exquisite, while the opposites, beakers with words like "hate," "war," and so on, appeared to be in a state of complete destruction. While it is difficult to measure love in any kind of quantitative way, there are increasing demonstrations, which have I coined as "Non-local Love," that are a very real phenomenon; something that mystics, artists, and visionaries have known and expressed forever.

Let me give you a little example I happened upon this morning. As I approached Starbucks toward the end of my walk, I wondered how I could best open the door with my cane in my right hand. Just then, a huge tattooed man who I had never seen before stepped beside me. He was dressed in black and smoking a cigarette. He looked like he was in his early twenties. "Pardon me, ma'am. I'd like to open the door for you," he said. And then, he did. You might think this is no big deal. But, as many seniors will attest, it is very unusual that elders are even noticed. (Often, walking down the street I encounter a 'gaggle' of teens so enthralled by one another that they block the entire road, oblivious that someone else needs to pass.)

It was this unexpected Non-Local Love that kept teaching me that our ideas about love are anemic. The question is: are you willing? Forget willpower. Just ask yourself, 'Am I willing' to experience more? Love? Life? Freedom?"

If you say "yes," and you practice what follows, without shortcuts, believe me, you will not only find your own Way (Buddhists call this the Middle Path, or The Way), but you will be more than happy to keep practicing. Remember that phrase, "Seek and ye shall find. Knock and the door shall be opened?" Doors are waiting for you, my friend. Are you willing to knock? Are you willing to practice? Join a sincere heart with practice and patience, and this is what will shift your life in the direction of loving relations with all things. Which, by the way, *includes you!*

Well, this is what you've got to do if you really want to have greater aliveness, abundance, and love in your life. You've got to seek it and open the door. You've got to knock. Believe this secret, for it is so!

Whatever door opens, whether it is tiny or tall, it is the right one for you as long as it delights your heart, regardless the life others tell you that you "should" be living. Your own Way of living Love is yours; custom-tailored to suit you and nobody else. This is how you come into harmonious meaningful connection with the world. Forget comparisons that lead you down another's road. Theirs will not work for you.

Recently, I was reminded of this. Having several dear friends wrapped up in doing podcasts and other public things, I started to think I should do that, as well. But I resisted, making many excuses. During my morning meditation, I was left with a familiar scene. In it, I was living on the edge of a village. At night, villagers would sneak to my hut, under the moonlight and stars, and secretly ask me for help. But this time, I remembered that part of my Shadow is ambition, a dragon I have fought off for many years. These sort of dragons are always born from fear. The belief that perhaps I should do what my friends were doing was seeded in ambition. Should I ever start doing a podcast, it will not be because I need to measure my worth by the outer world. That's all I am saying. We must live in accord with what it is, if well-framed, calls from our own heart.

Big or Small, It Does Not Matter

My own Way is small, for instance, but it is sincere. I love noticing the tiny things, the evidence of life flourishing that gets overlooked in the collective rush to be Somebody. I love making little expressions of love, creating things that have no outer world commercial value whatsoever, but are the exact things I like to gift. While I have a number of friends who live in the world of neon lights and worldly performances, including filling major stadiums, this has not been my own path. Some wonder why I take the time to construct works like this, to spend time and invest resources with and into people I might never meet in person, like you. People I might never hear from. I don't know.

Be the best possible steward to those seeds planted in your heart. This will lead you home.

Cara Barker

All I know is that the seeds of this desire were planted in my heart, and my job is to be the best possible steward of their growth. That's your job, too, although our metaphorical seeds are all unique. All I know is that you are here, right now. All I know is that you matter the world to me. All I know is that I've been at spots in my life when I wish someone would have heard me, would have shared their journey, would have offered their little map, would have familiarized me with the territory. For me, hearing not just from ears, but with my heart to another's story (not their bullshit story), is a great treasure. All I know is that we are here together, and I know there is a greater reason, if we are willing to be real.

Framing Our Real Truth Promotes Intimacy

I call my Path the way-of-into-me-see, or "intimacy." This is Love's way, through vulnerability, connection, and joy-based action. This means connecting with the light and beauty in all creation through our heart. It doesn't matter whether you call this good, or God, or if the very name "God" gives you the 'heebie jeebies,' throw an extra "o" into it, and that works too. I don't care what you call this higher, creative, invisible intelligence. That is not what matters. What does matter, however, if you want to build the strongest house for your best life is that you live the Love moving through you with each heartbeat audaciously. How do you do this? You begin practicing coming into good relations with all things. There's just no getting around it. Considering the best, strongest framing of the life you are building takes accurate measurement, endurance, and serious rest breaks.

Practice loving audaciously. Leave no stone unturned. Frame your more expansive way of living.

Cara Barker

Become a Person of Courage

Having the audacity to Love yourself in a world that's going bonkers, further and further along the road to its own destruction, by fanning intolerance and hate, is an act of bold and stunning courage. These days the news is flooded with horrific disasters. Just this week we saw the thousands of people killed in Libya, Maui, Ukraine, Israel, Palestine, and more around the world. And why? As a people, we have not been paying attention; we have not been good stewards to Mother Earth or all living things.

Let's face it. Nearly every movie and television show devotes itself to violence. No small wonder when we live in a culture which emphasizes and fixates on egregious acts of cruelty and mean-spiritedness. Increasingly, we witness an elevation of deviant behavior, mass shootings, and lack of fact finding and critical thinking. Sadly, this promotes an attitude that goes like this: It's not MY fault! The power of inspiration, hope, and heartfelt feelings is necessary if we are ever to frame, and then build, our best life.

We alone are left to choose. Either we make the choice to become a beaker of the Good, or one of destruction. As for me, there is but one life; this life is my life and this life is your life. This life comes from One Love that is the Source of who we are, and this means you, and this means now. So, yes, there is local love in your own vicinity that's familiar in form; a love with whom you have personal history. But, as I've pointed out, there is another Love, a Non-local Love, which transcends our capacity to understand it, much less dare to speak about it. Non-Local Love cannot be understood intellectually. Rather, comprehending Non-Local Love is experiential and intuitive. It is that sense that something invisible is at work on your behalf, attempting to guide your actions so that striving becomes more and more a thing of the past.

What Gets You Into Trouble Is Forgetting that You're Loved

When you forget this, you forget you are to express Love's life through you. You forget you were designed to express Good through serving those conditions that make you happiest. This is not that form of so-called service where you feel obliged or heavy if you refuse. Never forget that the Universe conspires to help you become its Love Project at work in the world, through how you serve a Greater Good.

Prescription

PART 1

This means that you are the first on your list to Love yourself more deeply, more consistently, than ever before. This means that you've got to take your own needs seriously. If you are exhausted, rest. If you are lonely, find someone to serve. If you are discouraged, locate someone who is even more down-hearted and reflect back to them what you are needing to hear. Practice loving audaciously! Leave no stone unturned. If you've been working too hard, come out to play. Take a chill pill. If you are a better giver than receiver, practice receiving. Start with the microscopic moments that move you. Love them with a grateful heart. Do these things over the next six weeks with a grateful heart. Watch what happens. Polish up your dancing shoes. If you are good to your word, if you really want more love in your life, you will be joining the happy dance, too! To do this you must have a more courageous conversation between your small-thinking and your own best self. To pull this off, you've got to throw off whatever leeches keep you chained to your old definition of yourself and your job.

Just last night, my friend of fifty years since grad school, by the name of Jane, and I sat on a park bench near the marina in Kirkland. Children were romping on the shore, the grown-ups were enjoying picnics on plaid blankets, and dogs were resting in the shade of oak trees. Across from us was a seventy-ish-year-old man in denim shorts and green and white stripe shirt dancing to the music a street artist was playing. The old man had absolutely no rhythm whatsoever. He reminded me of my husband dancing. But this guy, like Ed, loved music and danced like, as the saying goes, 'there was no tomorrow.' Awkward as he was, the sheer happiness he expressed was a gift for us beyond measure. How easy to judge. How courageous to dance when nobody else is joining in.

I saw a scene online that demonstrated this. In a large group, one man got up and started dancing. There was no music, he was just dancing to what was inside him. But it was not until a second person joined in that the crowd stopped laughing and started dancing. So, if nobody is 'dancing' to your inner song, no worries. All it takes is one more person to feel accompanied. *Perhaps this is why we authors and artists are so moved by hearing from those witnessing. Until then, our vulnerability is left hanging out like an old guy's beer belly.*

PART 2

The second part of your assignment, over these same next six weeks, is to make an appointment with yourself, for yourself, every single day, to enjoy the following guided imagery and track what comes to you from it each day. You will notice that some little true action step that you need to take to strengthen your skill and restore your confidence in practicing living your own heart-led life will arise from your heart. Write this step down each day and DO it. You are here, above everything else, to be the Love Project of something beyond your old identity.

If you are exhausted, rest. In fact, practice rest before you are tired!

Cara Barker

Prescribed Guided Imagery

Record the following, in your own voice, perhaps on your smart phone.

In a private place, become still, turning your attention to your breathing. When centered, say the following, *very* slowly, VERY SLOWLY, to yourself:

Let yourself be silently drawn by the stronger pull of what you really love.

Rumi

Breathing slowly in and out, relaxing your body . . . letting go of any lost love in the past . . . truly surrendering to the present moment . . . breathing in and out, relaxing every tiny muscle and every cell from the top of your head to the bottom of your toes, allowing your breath to remove any tension, any stress, each in-breath to restore new energy, new life.

Don't worry if you drift off to sleep . . . Your unconscious mind is very present, working on your behalf at all times, dropping into that deepest place inside you, the bridge to the very Source of Life which is moving through you. This greatest Wisdom is so all-encompassing that it knows precisely what is needed in the affairs of your life to bring about a Greater Good. Let go, now, of all your many concerns, releasing all your tensions to this Greater Good. Forget what your ego thinks you should be doing, knowing that all resources are coming your way. Let yourself be silently drawn by the stronger pull of what you really love.

You do not have to know how to solve old, stale relations, or those which are hurtful, including the ways you harm yourself, second-guess yourself, bully yourself . . . You are not alone, but rather, a Supreme Intelligence is always with you, in this moment, and this moment, and this moment, coming to your aid, moving through your body, releasing all toxins and signs of stress, making it much more comfortable to take a rest at last . . . to forgive yourself for what you've done, or have failed to do . . . to relieve yourself of carrying false burdens and obligations . . . to embrace that part of yourself that has allowed you to suffer at the hands of others and allowed you to be seduced by what has not served you. Yes, forgive yourself for the times you've forgotten you are loved, when you've forgotten that you are here, most importantly, as an instrument of a Greater Love, an outlet for a Greater Intelligence expressing Itself in the best possible ways.

Let yourself be silently drawn by the stronger pull of what you really love.

You can relax now, you can surrender all challenges and obstacles, all the mental clutter that keeps you from the freedom meant to be yours. And now, let yourself be silently drawn by the stronger pull of what you really love.

You are free, now, you are a part of a Greater Intelligence which has absolutely no barriers, no limits, nothing that it cannot move or resolve creatively. You let go of your focus on lack, on your perception of what is missing, or whatever is causing you distress. You are re-fastening your focus on what is larger than these concerns. You are reconnecting with loving resources that are coming your way more and more as you are opening your mind as never before . . . softening to your heart. to greater universal wisdom . . . enjoying what you are creating inside your heart, an atmosphere that is conducive to your complete relaxation . . . your complete sense of safety and reassurance.

Let yourself be silently drawn by the stronger pull of what you really love.

You find yourself breathing in and breathing out all that comforts and renews your faith in a Greater Love, a local and Non-Local Love, and you rest in this natural great peace . . . allowing all thoughts of lack, all feelings of fear just melt away, like snowflakes on a warm window pane. Breathing in and breathing out kindness for yourself, for the you that has suffered in the basement of your unconscious, knowing that even this aspect of your being is trying to help you in its own way . . . and so you thank this part of yourself that's been hurting too long, mistrusting too long.

Breathing in and out, you allow this wounded one to take a long-overdue rest . . . to really rest now, in the heart of love. And you continue breathing in and out down to the very core, the very essence of your being, your cells, where new life is being conceived with every new healthy thought. Breathing in and out your own movement, your own growing.

Let yourself be silently drawn by the stronger pull of what you really love.

Softly noticing the footprints that have been drawing you toward what you really love . . . which have brought you to this moment. You are cherishing the courage behind these many footprints . . . your own courage . . . the courage of those who've gone before you, your people's people. And you see that each of you were called into Life at the time that each was needed as a recording instrument of the audacity of Love, doing its best to express Itself through your people, to the best of their abilities . . . in their own unique and necessary ways . . . to tell the human story. You are breathing in and breathing out gratitude.

Let yourself be silently drawn by the stronger pull of what you really love.

Not only the people you've known, but even strangers, who, through their example, have reminded you of what matters most to your heart.

You allow yourself to drift downward into your center even more, and as you do so, you sense an entire world within you. A cosmos of which you are a part, and in which you reside, informing one another of all that wants to come to life. You are feeling this movement, this dance of Life of which you are a part. You allow your heart to fill up and overflow with those desires, those wishes which bring you the deepest sense of aliveness . . . the deepest sense of joy. And you notice that very gently . . . way, way far back on the horizon of your creative imagination . . . there is an order out of the chaos forming something that brings you great joy at the very prospect.

Let yourself be silently drawn by the stronger pull of what you really love.

And you are noticing that this very order connects you with a Higher Presence, an eternal and bold Love whose sole purpose is to express your heart's desire through your life. You are arriving at a place of deepest peace where there is nothing whatsoever for you to do. Your only job is to receive in this present moment, to let this be your focus . . . your surrender . . . your true relationship with what is greater and more generous than you can imagine. From this place, you feel something within your deepest make-up that longs for fuller expression in your life . . .and it is Good . . . and it comes from a greater good   and you are a reflection and child of this Greater Good . . . you are here on Its behalf.

Let yourself be silently drawn by the stronger pull of what you really love.

Remember the statement:

"For where your treasure is, there your heart will be also."
Matthew 6:21

I once heard a Chinese proverb in Singapore which says:

If you want happiness for an hour, take a nap.

If you want happiness for a day, go fishing.

If you want happiness for a year, receive a rich inheritance.

If you want happiness for a lifetime, help someone.

What face comes to your mind right now? Who would benefit

from your heart expressing itself gently, in some little, tiny, tender, helpful way?

'If you want happiness for a lifetime, help someone,' says the proverb.

Dropping deeply down into a field of complete calm and utter peace . . . the place beyond your little personality, the place where you discover and witness; witness Wisdom expressing Her beautiful self in you. Drop down into your heart, breathe in, breathe out, and notice what arises from your heart to these inquiries:

Where has your love become too small?

What is your heart hoping to find through your life right now?

What is your heart wanting you to discover that could help you step out of the box you've been in?

To what are you drawn right now, what do you really love right now?

END MEDITATION

Keep track of your findings. Once a week for the following six weeks record your findings in three sentences or less in a journal or in the space provided in the back of this book, and add a suggested action step, as well as what this opened up for you. You will be tempted to scrap this exercise in self-compassion. Value yourself and do it anyway! .

Week 1 What I'm finding in my heart is the hope for:

_____

_____

_____

The little action step I need to take today to love myself better is:

_____

_____

_____

My mind is opening to the possibility for love to express itself through:

_____

_____

_____

The body is purified by water.
The ego is purified by tears.
The intellect is purified by knowledge.
The Soul is purified by love.

Imam Ali

CHAPTER 40

Finding Love Through True Relations

As you progress through the next six weeks, using the previous exercise every day and recording your findings, you will gain more clarity, more self-compassion. Increasingly, you will find essential answers for your homecoming. For example, "To what are you drawn right now, what do you really love right now?"

For me, the stronger pull toward what I really love IS love. I love love! What I mean by that is the rare opportunity to be completely present in the moment. Sounds simple, I know. But it has taken the long road home for me to arrive at something so true for me throughout my life. It is, however, an inconvenient truth in this world with its obsession over possessions, lottery tickets, and stocks. Nature, and Her surprises, is a good starter place early in the day. For example: today I saw a green and a red throated hummingbird fly atop my evergreen tree. The moment was yummy.

A Word About Love

Love is not only what makes the "world go round," or sells Hallmark cards on Valentine's Day. Love is the glue that repairs broken hearts, dreams, and connections. Love is the stuff that reminds you that you are not only connected, but you, yourself, are Love. In fact, developing true relations brings you sooner or later to the realization that you are here, in this life, in this precise situation on "your plate" today, with this exact circle of people involved, in order to become a distributor of a Greater Good through employing your love and its gifts into service in those exact ways that make you happiest.

Remember, love is not a noun, actually. It is a verb; a dynamic energy in motion. Even when I speak of it, I think of it as a flowing river. Moving, ever moving, sometimes blocked by a 'logjam,' i.e., fear of being too vulnerable.

But then, Love is bold. Love is focused. Love is Wisdom. Love persists, even when the little mind falls into doubt. At the end of the day, what really matters most gets down to Love. Love forgives. Love cherishes. Love heals. Love reminds you that you are never alone, that you are Its instrument . . . here to spread it around . . . here to begin the process of reconciliation—to come back home to your heart-led life. You are to realign your actions with laying those four essential cornerstones, beginning with clearing your mind of the limiting thoughts in your way before you dig down deep to your core nature, then taking the trouble to make sure the foundation you are laying for your expanded life is solid, and third, taking your time building the firmest frame to support the fourth cornerstone the building of you. (The fourth cornerstone is up ahead). Your love connects those around you and connects you with what's within your innermost heart. Love converts the hardened and restores light in the darkest corners. Love unites, it does not separate. Love discerns, it does not dissipate. Love fertilizes and nourishes, it never starves. Love uplifts. Someone needs your love today. Look in the mirror, for openers. Start there. Have you told the one in the mirror what you love especially about you today? Why not? Take a break and do it now. No joke. No guts, no glory.

Prescription

If you haven't done this, stop. You can take time to go to the restroom and privately look at the one in the mirror (if you are at work, etc.). Take your time. When you've taken the time to "love on yourself," come back and describe what you're noticing. Complete the following to have a more honest, joyful, and courageous conversation with the beautiful creature inside you.

I'm noticing that the person in the mirror:

appreciates

_____

would like

_____

enjoys

_____

questions

_____

wishes

_____

would love

_____

Reader Instructions

Now that you have filled in these blanks, use the same format over the next six weeks on the journal pages in this book or in your own notebook. Make sure you date your entries and take time to include the details of your observations for best results.

What is audacious Love to you? What are the little signs and pieces of evidence that Love teaches you over the next six weeks? Let me know! Write me at carabarker.com. or alternately dr.carabarker@gmail.com.

I'm listening. And don't forget to include the best expression of love you've ever experienced! Don't forget to mention what you're loving about that person in the mirror. I want to know. Love starts with the first things first. Practice this mirror exercise at least four times a day, every day, for the next six weeks. Be prepared. You are going to attract some beautiful experiences and have a greatly enriched experience of moving home to your best Self. Practice this six-week exercise faithfully, and the meaning of true relations of Love will become apparent. You will open up to a new way of defining the experience, framing, and even learn a new way of spelling it. Try it out on paper.

What does L O V E mean? Play with vertical spelling. I'll show you mine:

Here's the way I spell love vertically:

L= Liberation (of the)

O= One Life, (the) One

V= Voice (you and I have for)

E= Expressing (Its light, for the greater good, through our life)

Practicing your Love with audacity teaches us the most important things. Chief among them are those moments and actions, those true relations, which bring you to life. Said David Whyte at a commencement address at Pacific Lutheran University in Tacoma:

> "What are the things that keep us alive? Thousands of voices calling you to be many things, but the one thing you were called here to be. The question is when the tide of fortune turns against you, can you remember who you truly are? Like Shakespeare, much of the time we must look at the story we are telling ourselves and ask whether it is big enough. You must have taken vows for something larger than what you are being, doing and having. . . . One of the ways we protect ourselves from failure is to turn away from our dreams. We must chance it. What have been your repeating dreams? What was central to this repeating theme?"

When I heard this and reflected upon David's words with regard to my own experience, I felt like I was being handed gold: a sort of teacher's answer sheet at the end of the book, where I was being given the test questions and could prepare myself for examination when I got my own "walking papers." Now, you've got them, too.

So, as you move along your own path, do so informed. Know that your desert is not the end of the road, but a means, if consciously faced, to deepen your connection with what you love, and how you wish to serve this Great Good, this One Love, with all your heart. One of the benefits of aging consciously is that we get closer to our own body's impermanence. We no longer fantasize that we have forever. Freely translated, it means we know in our gut that we better 'get cracking.' We cannot luxuriate in the fantasy that death is far in the future.

As you travel through your own desert facing your own blockage (limited beliefs) and find the first symbolic, or literal, trickle of water, the first inkling that you are in the vicinity of a greater Love than you've ever known, a Love of which you are an integral part, receive this moment with a grateful heart. You are on your way. In fact, if you want to practice in a way that produces the most enduring results, begin expressing a grateful heart before you find what you've been wanting. This has a magnetic way of attracting really interesting, good things. All I know for certain is that doing so has worked for moi and others I know.

But, be forewarned! If you are accustomed to striving and driving to get what you want, this will get in your way of practicing a grateful heart. The stress and strain of will-powering, your way to what you desire will leave precious little room for Life Force to assist you. So, and please forgive me for being bossy, but here goes: stop white-knuckling it, stop striving, stop struggling. Sure, up to a certain point, independence will help you build confidence, but if you want to create what's beyond any one person's ability, you had better give it a rest. Open yourself to a much more enjoyable ride. Remember what I told you before, that the Universe conspires to help you? Well, you've got to practice leaving room for the unexpected to arrive. Warning: know this does not happen with a snap of your fingers. If you've ever watched the construction of large houses, you can attest to the fact that most of the time is spent constructing the foundation. So too here, we are moving through our obstacles and liberating our homemade story of how life is supposed to work.

Prescription

Practice the following simple exercise until you no longer think of it as an assignment but do it automatically for the benefit it brings. Upon awakening, and before dropping off to sleep, aloud or in writing, express your gratitude. Simply repeat and fill in the sentence until you feel complete. Feel free to do this as an ongoing recording below, in your journal or the pages at the back of the book.

I am grateful for

_____

I am grateful for

_____

I am grateful for

_____

I am grateful for

_____

I am grateful for

_____

I am grateful for

_____

I am grateful for

_____

Remember, you are not here to figure out all the details by yourself. Hanging onto them will only create more strain in your system. Trust me, I know this to be true! I see this at work in my own life, through my family, and certainly in the lives of clients, students, and friends. It's impossible to figure out how your heart's desire is going to materialize, and the many details that will come together to make it so.

Just the other night, I happened to come across a piece of writing that I did in 1979, in which I described my heart's desire and how I wished to serve and live. It was just what I wanted. What I also recorded was that I had no clue how, or if, such a life would ever be possible. So, I turned it over, and went about my business.

Today, as I reread that description, every facet of what I desired has come to life; this life that is my life. But, to tell you the truth, I have no idea of how it all came to pass. I just followed my nose and took the next best step before me according to the inaudible whisper of my heart, not my head. Had I only paid attention to my head's need to 'be miserable' like a walking corpse, none of what has developed would have come to pass.

Some people prefer to make 'vision boards,' meaning collecting pictures that illustrate what you want in your life and gluing them onto a background. I was lukewarm on the idea, but I made one and put it in our garage, so when I did the elliptical, I saw it every day for one and a half years. Recently, I dusted it off. Every single image had concretized itself in my life, without me ever thinking about the board! Clearly, the unconscious was absorbing it every day when I spent forty-five minutes on the elliptical.

It's best to follow your intuition. There's a wisdom in it. Even my greatest losses and disappointments turned out to be steppingstones necessary to building my own heart-led life. (Even my present need for knee replacements, which seem to have thrown a monkey wrench into this whole upcoming year, I trust as part of my curriculum.)

You see, we just never know. But, as Sara Lawrence-Lightfoot pointed out in the third chapter, those who write out on paper the life they want to be living, when they are in transition, do far better than those who do not. The outcome has nothing to do with moving into that "make it happen" mentality. This bad habit only taxes your sympathetic nervous system and brings restlessness and insomnia. Whenever you get trapped in the bad habit of overdoing it, like the one-armed paper hanger, know that you've slipped into temporary amnesia, pretending you are not 'good enough.'

Radical Restructuring

That's why I will encourage you again and again to practice listening to your heart's deepest desire, every single day. Practice writing it down, as redundant as this may seem; you may think it's stupid, or overkill, or like 'beating a dead horse.' You are worth the time, my friend. Take one tiny true action step in that direction.

Warning: this requires turning a deaf ear to the outer world, diving into the silence of the inner as your guide, and paying attention to your dreams, symptoms, and what seems like chance but are actually meaningful happenings. Turn the rest of the details over to the One Life that is greater than you or me. Let Life hold the details for you. STOP STRIVING. Do your best, and, as a buddy of mine says, "Leave the rest." Just focus on what holds your heart in this and all your moments. Do this with your whole heart and an open mind. The rest will take care of itself. We're talking radical restructuring here. This means that to build a better life, we've got to be honest with ourselves and listen quietly to our heart. You can forget all your ideas and theories about what whole-hearted living is and release them, because they won't help. What will help, and it is the only thing that will help, is your conscious choice to discover what it means to be in true relations with your heart's desire, living it to the hilt. Making it concrete. Let yourself be a convert to the one true life that is Love. Don't get scared on me, now! Conversion simply means turning in the direction of turning over your heart.

An illustration

Twenty-nine years ago, according to my journal, I was literally, psychologically, spiritually, and workwise in the desert. My husband's work had necessitated a move, and I was angry. At first, I felt like a victim, not an attractive place to be. So, I made this choice. I did not know where this life shift would lead, but eventually I woke up, realizing that rearrangement of my life was some sort of teaching. I turned my head around and slowly began to trust the process. I did not know what this would mean tomorrow, or in the next five minutes. All I knew was that the only thing that seemed to be helping was to move in the direction Love was leading me and become its dance partner. Resentment and victimization were grinding me down and away from a deeper way of living that became healing.

One early morning, around 5:00 a.m., near the man-made lake I'd found on a walk in Arizona, something started to break through my rigid thinking . . . something I would not have imagined: little tunes, complete with lyrics. Never mind that I wasn't a singer! The songs would just stream through me as though a faucet was open. They came so fast and furiously I couldn't keep up with them. Somewhere, I've got a little tape of them to this day (no doubt hiding in some moving box.) On that particular day, out in the desert, my idea about who I was and what I was here to do went through the shredder!

All stress comes about through resistance to change.

Judge Thomas Troward

Love has a way of strip-searching our opinions and beliefs about ourselves that hold us back. Love has a powerful way of peeling away who we aren't, revealing something fresh. At first, this means tolerating feeling good and raw. I did not know at the time, and it's a good thing I didn't, that this musical experience would lead me to Asia, where, unwittingly, I'd find myself "streaming'" more impromptu little songs to groups with whom I was working. Eventually, this led me to not only some much-needed singing lessons, but another Master Teacher by the name of Cora Jackson, who loves audacity as much as I do.

Love has a way of guiding us to the very next step and Source we need. Remember how Rumi puts it?

> "Let yourself be silently drawn by the stronger pull of what you really love."

When you do, be prepared. I'm telling you! This will strip you down to the nitty gritty, so to speak. But do it anyway! Let's hear Rumi one more time:

> "Let yourself be silently drawn by the stronger pull of what you really love."

Why the strip down? To find out this one truth: you and I are, in a sense, like an onion, needing to peel away layers and layers of limiting beliefs and costumes. Yes, some might make your eyes water. But at our core is something magnificent: our true nature, designed to make the world kinder, more patient, and more compassionate in an original way. You are an instrument of divine expression. Not that you don't feel divine most of the time! Not that you don't doubt your beauty, your wisdom, your Love, for this is part of the human predicament. We forget. But just because we forget does not mean that more is not possible. Not just the "more" of acquisition, but, frankly, the "stuff" of possessions is just the training wheels for the curriculum of the real "more." This more has to do with living your own Truth wholeheartedly, following the thread to your own heart's delight without the need to question, doubt, or diminish what is embedded within your deepest core. There is a Truth inside you that carries the capacity to set you free.

What will help you move with greater ease toward freedom? Albert Einstein answered it this way, "You cannot solve a problem at the level of the problem."

To move toward liberation, in framing the life you are creating, you've got to be willing to break through self-imposed limits. Yes, you've got to be willing to identify your heart's desire. Search for it (I used to think mine were just hobbies.) You've got to be willing to follow the direction of your delight, trusting this to be your ethical duty to your own Soul. Judge Thomas Troward says something that you need to remember plainly: "The First thing in any investigation is to have some idea of what you are looking for—to have at least some notion of the general direction in which to go—just as you would not go up a tree to find fish, though you would for bird's eggs."

The moment we move in this wise direction, we enter transition, where the unimaginable may be found. Here's where the eggs are waiting; the protected secret for the life you wish to be living.

But first, the leap, facing the fear of getting hurt. For more often than not, we get shoved out of the comfy familiar by the Universe whether we like it or not.

. . . . She said: 'Come to the edge.'
Her babies cried out: 'We can't. We are afraid.'
Again, She said: 'Come to the edge.'
'No, no, it's too scary.'
So She pushed.
And they flew.

                                        Author unknown

CHAPTER 41

Finding Your Heart's Desire During Transitional Times

If we allow ourselves to complete the process, profound transition times lead to what is sometimes called the inner Sophia. Called by many names throughout the ages, your "Sophia" is your innermost wisdom; the feminine face of Creative Intelligence who Solomon praised. The "Sophia" guides you along your journey . . . if you listen! But this is neither the all nor is it novel. As we go to this place, we are drawn closer to humanity and our interconnection with all that is natural and love for all beings at a time on the planet when humanity is in dire crisis. Yet still, it is hard sometimes to wish for the best for tyrants. The movement is crucial: to deepen how we feel, expanding our relationship and world via meditation, prayers, and sacred practices. All three must be developed if you want to frame more out of life.

There was nothing new about the demonstrations of this non-local Love that day, years ago, which I described to you earlier during my "desert period," nor in those that followed. According to scholar Robert Morrow:

> Over the course of history, there have been revelations of the Divine Sophia, Mother of Humanity, the one who guides us in the unfolding of evolution, who has revealed Herself, given revelations of Herself to different people of the earth, different

traditions and religions everywhere. She's revealed Herself in all religions, Christianity, Judaism, Buddhism, Taoism, Muslim and so on, Hinduism. . . . King Solomon was an archetypal seeker of Sophia . . . a thousand years before the birth of Christ. . . . Through Her, he opened his heart to Creation. This is possible through prayer, meditation, and being more aware of the world around us, every tree, mountain, lake can speak to us of Divine Sophia, of the love that weaves through the world, how open hearts can have conversation. . . . Mysticism is not something confined to a few great mystics, but is our God-given inheritance to appreciate the world through our hearts, to appreciate everything, and allow our hearts to speak in a profound way. . . . The Temple of Solomon was testimony to Divine Wisdom and love. The building of it was something illustrating what is potential for all of us if we will open and align our minds, hearts and will to what is greater than our own.

These encounters, be they through sacred dreaming, instincts, or compelling attractions, point the way to your unique path and contribution to come. They can help you come into real connection and conversation with your best self if your ego will surrender. Your biggest task during your transition is opening to mysterious demonstrations while keeping your feet on the ground and your wits about you. The truth is that concrete demonstrations of love are unfolding all around us all the time. It is your choice whether or not to get rid of what flattens your experience of life today and keeps you thirsty and starving for what might actually nourish your Soul.

. . . the problem is not entirely in finding a room of one's own. The time alone, difficult and necessary as this is, the problem is more how to still the soul in the midst of its activities . . . how to feed the soul . . . For it is the Spirit . . . that is going dry.

Anne Morrow Lindberg

Jung described his own life-changing encounter of learning to have a heart for himself in his private *The Red Book* in this way:

> . . . . Give me your hand, my almost forgotten Soul. How warm the joy at seeing you again, you long, disavowed Soul. Life has led me back to you. Let us thank the life I have lived for all the happy and the sad hours, for every joy, for every sadness. My Soul, my journey should continue with you . . . . I still labored misguidedly under the Spirit of this time, and thought and spoke much of the Soul. I knew many learned words for Her, and turned Her into a scientific object. I did not consider that my Soul cannot be the object of my judgment and knowledge . . . . Therefore, the Spirit of the Depths forced me to speak to my Soul, to call upon Her as a living and self-existing being. I had to become aware that I had lost my Soul . . . . I had to accept that what I had previously called my Soul was not my Soul at all, but a dead system. Hence I had to speak to my Soul as to something far off and unknown, which did not exist through me, but through whom I existed. " . . . . He whose desire turns away from outer things, reaches the place of the Soul . . . .

Two questions come to mind when I read this:

(1) What is the Spirit of our time? From where I sit it looks like violence, new iterations of virus, anger, despair, homelessness, loneliness, consumerism, fighting, division, and fear of anything that is considered 'other.'

(2) To what is your own Soul calling? That is: how do you turn toward this "place of the Soul?" Do you want to know?

CHAPTER 42

Building a More Solid Frame by Listening To Your Heart

Jung's description provides a guidepost for your next step. If you want more love expressed through your life, cultivate a "heart" toward yourself. This is one of the best-kept secrets that stops most of us from getting more out of life. So, let me repeat: cultivate a heart for yourself. Why is it that we might love others, be kind as needed, yet deny ourselves the same courtesy? Turn in this direction.

By way of example, my neighbor, Darla, a true angel in human form, came to my door unasked, and took away an outdoor rug that was dangerous, especially with my knees these days, then took the trash down the ramp to dispose of it along with the rug. While leaving, Darla said, "I'll come back tomorrow to help you water."

None of this was done at my request. Simply put, she was present. She noticed. She took action. This is how she dances with life.

Begin in little ways. Maybe this morning you are struck by the freshness of the air. Perhaps you are on the cusp of a new season. Maybe instead of rushing to the car, you pause for a moment, indulging your Spirit, "feeding" your Soul, nourishing your sense of well-being. Taking time assists your navigation through times of chaos. Nourish your Soul by moving toward what "feeds" you. Naturally, we rarely feel called to do so unless a crisis arrives and nothing else works. In this sense, desperation carries a gift that Pema Chodron, a marvelous Buddhist-teaching nun, discusses:

> "It is fairly common for crisis and pain to connect people with their capacity to love and care about one another. It is also common that this openness and compassion fades rather quickly, and that people then become afraid and far more guarded and closed than they were ever before. The question, then, is not only how to uncover our fundamental tenderness and warmth, but also how to abide there with the fragile, often bittersweet vulnerability? How can we relax and open to the uncertainty of it?"

How, indeed? Breathe one breath at a time. Learn to meditate. Experiment with whatever form fits for you. Perhaps "sitting meditation" is not "your thing." Explore, then, engaged meditation, where you become mindful to relax all inner chatter, maybe through slow walking, painting, knitting, gardening, coloring, or doodling. You get the drift.

Prescription

Fill in the following:

What relaxes me is:

_____

_____

What clears my mind best is:

_____

_____

What opens my heart is:

_____

_____

What I haven't tried yet (but am curious) which would support my own vulnerability:

_____

_____

CHAPTER 43

Reach Out and Touch

It is man's task, his greatest task, not to learn to love, but to learn how to create the conditions in which love can alight upon us and remain with us. It is not what we know that heals, but how, with space, intention, and time, we prepare the atmosphere for love to arrive.

I received a demonstration of this through an important dream. Before falling asleep, I had laid out my clothes for a trip to London the following day. I was so excited because I had an appointment with a man I adored by the name of Sir Laurens van der Post, and afterward, we would be sharing dinner. The previous year, Sir Laurens and I had begun conversations having to do with connection, belonging, and what we had come to call "wholeheartedness" in our journeys home to who we really are. I cherished the sharing, the opportunity for cross-cultural learning, and the inspiration. That night I had a dream where Sir Laurens told me that his "walking papers" had come. Meaning, he was moving on, and before he went, he wanted to leave me with instructions about writing that he urged me to do. (I wasn't so sure, but he kept insisting anyway.) He showed me how the writing I had to do must evolve from a particular sacred practice. The instructions were specific. The next morning, after my shower, the news came on the radio that Sir Laurens had died hours earlier. I have done my best to practice the wisdom of this dream ever since. But what this taught me is that Love lives on in non-local ways. Love transcends what we believe is possible to the degree we are willing to give and receive.

When we complete the journey to our own heart, we will find ourselves in the hearts of everyone else.

Father Thomas Keating

In the years since then, researchers are finding that well-being is most strengthened within positive, supportive, forward-moving communities. If you want more real connection through your way of living, then be discerning. Choose wisely, move in the direction of those who cherish life and are grateful, willing to learn, and "ageless." Get rid of the toxic people in your life. You don't need them.

Says Mary Catherine Bateson:

> One of the things we know about the human capacity to keep on learning, to remain young at the heart, and willing to learn, is that it needs to be supported by cherishing. We need to be cherished as infants, and as adults we need to cherish our children. But if we want a society of people willing and open and ready to learn, it has to be a kinder, gentler society, because we need a lot of mutual support to face change, to give up things we've always believed in.

Turning within during the toughest times, when people give you unsolicited advice, you may think you are alone. You can play the 'lone ranger,' but it will not advance you in the direction of your dreams. For that, we need to expand and deepen our participation within a community that supports the essence of its members.

Prescription

If you could "design" the perfect "cherishing community for you," what would it include? Describe it in detail here:

_____

_____

_____

_____

Do NOT cheat yourself. If you bypassed this prescription, go back. Remember, taking the time to write down your intention has a power in it. Your neural pathways are 'listening.' Cherish yourself. This is a prerequisite to attracting a fuller cherishing community. By way of example, just last night on my neighbor Darlene's deck, after a late dinner, I became deeply moved by her ways of giving. Instantly I knew she was part of my Soulful community.

Want to know a secret? You cannot move forward 'on your lonesome.' Sure, we must take ownership of our lives and take action steps that are our own to take. However, this is not enough if you want more out of life. You are a part, an integral part, of a bigger chorus. For example, just this morning on the news was a story about an organization called Champions for Change. This group gathers together to sing. Big deal, right? Yes, it is. Each member has dementia or Alzheimer's. Their music in the company of others so challenged brings them to life. The arts are medicinal.

CHAPTER 44

Meeting and Greeting the "Newborn"

Most of us are not 'wolf children.' We were not left alone in the forest, abandoned to be raised by wolves. Most of us had help. Maybe it wasn't perfect help or a nourishing environment, but whoever was there did the best they could based on their level of understanding about what a newborn needs, and likewise their self-awareness. From the beginning of life, and throughout, to flourish, we need connection and help in holding what is dear to our heart and Soul.

The Need for Swaddling

During an identity upheaval, there's a profound need to attend to the needs of the newborn: the unexpected expansion of personality. Just as a neonate needs to feel secure boundaries, so do we during edge times. Making art has always been a form of psychic swaddling for me during states of developmental reinvention. It has helped me "draw a line" between the old and the new, draw a bridge to what I need, draw upon larger resources, draw out what wants to come to life inside of me. It neither matters "why" this is, nor whether we consider ourselves talented. I've passed this along to more non-artists than artists because it works if you 'take the prescription.'

Whatever image arises, you might want to think it's stupid. For example, what I doodled just now was a red geranium. Huh? But then this image revealed to me that it can keep blooming, assuming I nourish it on a regular basis. What this also means is dead-heading the old. Our psyche (Soul) is so wise! Just now I asked myself what nourishment is needed? The answer: lunch!

Prescription

In your journal or on a page in the back of this book, please do the following:

1. You can simply "doodle" whatever image your creative imagination brings out. Ask your unconscious mind to help you doodle a sketch of what's being born through you. Use your non-dominant hand. No one needs to see it.

2. Now, add to the figure something that would suggest increased safety, joy, playfulness, or spontaneity.

3. On the back, write down the first three words that come to you. Date your doodle.

4. What clue is this giving you about your evolving self? What inside of you is hoping you'll provide for its unfolding?

5. How, specifically, can you show more compassion toward this part of yourself, which you need to do before you can feel more compassion for others? Identify three specific doable steps:

Step #1

_____

Step # 2

_____

Step # 3

_____

CHAPTER 45

Protecting the Emerging Self

If you've ever been around a newborn, you know that it's crucial to protect this little one because neither it's immune system nor the top part of the skull are fully mature. We do not hand our newborns to strangers. We protect and swaddle the little one. We hold it close. We nourish it. We provide quiet and rest. We avoid anything that will overtax the baby, for doing so supports growth. Why is it, then, that when you are undergoing a significant life change, you do not cherish yourself as much? Why do you place yourself in situations that do not provide enough tender regard for yourself and leave you so depleted? You are drained because you are investing your life energy in the wrong things. Stop it! Go only into those situations where there is genuine sense of meeting. Protecting your emerging self is an exercise in setting better boundaries; saying "no, thank you" more, and "yes" less. Only in this way can you meet what lays hidden in the heart beneath the intellect.

Prescription
Complete Parts A through D below to begin to build better boundaries.

PART A:

List ten things you do that drain your energy. Don't censor yourself.

1.

_____

_____

2.

_____

_____

3.

_____

_____

4.

_____

_____

5.

_____

_____

6.

_____

_____

7.

_____

_____

8.

_____

_____

9.

_____

_____

10.

_____

_____

PART B:

Put an asterisk beside each item in Part A that could be delegated. To do this, you must be willing to let go of the need for control and perfection.

PART C:

To each item, add the name of a person, organization, or problem-solver who could assist you in delegating that task.

PART D:

List the three things which you would most enjoy saying "yes" to.

1.

_____

2.

_____

3.

_____

Now relist them in rank order.

1.

_____

2.

_____

3.

_____

Protecting the emerging self requires cultivation and discernment for not only what you choose to do and not to do, but for those with whom you choose to meet and collaborate. Consider the following following from Irene de Castillego:

> We are only exhausted when talking to other people if we do not meet them, when one or both of them are hiding behind screens. On the rare occasions when we are fortunate enough to truly meet someone, there is no question of fatigue. Both are refreshed, something has happened. It is as though a door had opened, and life suddenly takes on new meaning. Why is it we meet so seldom?

Prescription

List four names of people who leave you feeling refreshed and joyful.

1.

_____

2.

_____

3.

_____

4.

_____

Reflect on your list. What's the shared theme or quality of these people that is conducive to your well-being and development? Write this out if you really want value:

_____

Perhaps what Irene de Castillejo says will resonate:

> For there to be a meeting, it seems as though a third, a some-thing else, is always present. You may call it Love or the Holy Spirit, Jungians would say it is the Presence of the Self. If this Other is present, there cannot have failed to be a meeting . . . .

Prescription

Briefly describe a time when, while meeting deeply in the moment with someone truly present, you had a sense of other, or the beloved, in your midst:

_____

_____

_____

Meetings, such as the one you described, have a hidden secret healing power in them. From this underground comes the wisdom of sages, artists, visionaries, and children.

Just the other day, at the Safeway checkout, a four-year-old little boy came up to me and said, "This is the most awesome day of my whole life!"

He had the wisdom to notice. His truth, simply shared, helped to remind me what encourages new life can be the simplest of meetings with the fewest of words.

Healing only happens when you meet on the deepest, most essential level. This is the heart level, which is usually is voiceless and silent. This came to me most poignantly a few weeks after my son died when I received an unexpected package in the mail. Paula, who sent the package, included a brief note that read: "I have no idea what to say. I cannot imagine losing my boy. So, I sat with my experience and thought of you with each of these pictures."

Enclosed was a notebook filled with many, many scenes. It was tremendously touching, connecting, and healing. It also offered me the needed space between words to simply "be." Or, as The Beatles put it: "Let It Be."

The challenge is not lingering at either extreme. Too much focus on the rational can annihilate our metaphorical river of feelings (as opposed to emotions). Too much of the latter kills off innate heart wisdom. Too much of the former blocks wise action in the world.

Women in today's world are thrown into the masculine way of focused consciousness, which pulls us away from our heart knowledge. The push to rush, plan, and succeed silences wisdom, log-jamming a sense of its flow, rhythm, beauty, and love. We need transition spaces from one way of being to the next. But the underlying need, my friend, is to practice the necessary practices, learn the necessary skills to awaken your Love wisdom 24/7, and follow it to the letter! Dream interpretation can be deeply meaningful.

Albert Schweitzer once said:

"Until he extends his circle of compassion to all living things, man will not himself find peace."

We must begin with ourselves and the unmet emerging self.

Beginning with yourself, however, takes the temptation to live as we always have, without the courage to evolve. What Dr. Jung said is true. Paraphrasing it, our greatest stumbling block is indifference. Too many marriages go on for years with nary a spark of new life. Think of the marital partner who begins sleeping with his back to his partner.

Man's greatest passion is apathy.

Carl Jung

So, what happens when we fail to do this? Turn the page to see.

CHAPTER 46

The Killing Thing

It is not anger that kills building a more loving life; it is indifference. Be it indifference to your partner, your parent, your child, or your creative act of self-expression, it kills because it cuts off connection with Life Force. The most destructive thing is when you are indifferent to the hidden you that needs to come forth. When you are indifferent to what delights your heart most, you lose your way back home. Here's how I see it, in a piece that came to me. I call it:

It All Gets Down To Love

Bread, no matter how you slice it, is bread.

Life, no matter how it changes, it all gets down to love.

Sure, we set our goals establish our intention.

But, in the end, what matters to your heart?

It all gets down to love.

Regardless of what gets accomplished, regardless of how many things you have to check off of your to do list today, what really matters?

None of these, nor the obligations they carry,

Even come close to the value of 'It all gets down to love.'

At the end of the day,

And the end of the race,

I am accountable to answer the questions: How did I love today?

How did I serve that love?

It all gets down to love.

Love pays attention. Love is not indifferent, passive, or hesitant. When readers respond to your writing or when listeners respond to your creation, such an intentional act is a demonstration of love through compassion, empathy, connection, self-worth, and generosity. Love is not a bystander. Love gets out of the bleachers and into the game. Love stands up, speaks out, and shines a light in the darkness. Love illuminates life, supporting it to flow through your own unfolding story. Love requires response.

Whatever Love is, there is a powerful force behind it: there is good. Recently, as a featured contributor for the *Huffington Post*, I wrote a series that had to do with love and loss. Many readers wrote in describing their incredible experiences and lessons learned, one of which had to do with the awkward dilemma of how to express love at times of personal upheaval. From this "conversation," a green bracelet was designed. Whenever they are given out, we say:

"My love is with you; my heart is with you."

Feel free to create these bracelets yourself, especially if you never know the right words to say in the face of someone else's grief (there aren't any). The most important thing at such times is your presence.

This responsive simple act is one of many Love Projects underway. May love bloom beautifully in the garden of your heart.

My wish for you: may your life be a living, building, heart-led life.

How has a recent responsiveness (that warmed your heart) demonstrated love for you?

The situation:

_____

_____

The result:

_____

_____

How could you respond in a meaningful way to someone else this week?

_____

_____

Prescription

Recall a time when an issue arose that was inconvenient, yet someone responded in a way that touched your heart, and maybe even surprised you. Describe it here:

_____

_____

CHAPTER 47

Why You Must Give Up Trying So Hard

Think back to a time when you wanted something desperately. Perhaps what you wanted was a more loving relationship. Recall when you wanted whatever you wanted so much that you fell into a counterproductive effort of working too hard to create it.

If you are part of the crew I have coined as the "world weary," (see *World Weary Woman: Her Wound and Transformation*) listen up. Realize that entering a fuller relationship with who you are at core is not accomplished by more striving. Quite the contrary. When we try too hard to create what we want, we're not trusting our heart's silent guidance. Before you know it, we turn ourselves into a pretzel, twisting and turning, silencing and abandoning our own truth. This is because we believe striving is the key. It isn't.

Hope deferred makes the heart sick.

Proverbs 13:22

A few days ago, on my daily walk, I passed by another building site, the construction crew arguing with the builder. The latter was confronting the men with anger. With quite an attitude, he told them that the entrance to the home was "all wrong." Said one of the men confronted: "Sir, no disrespect, but the beam will not be symmetrical. It will not work. I'm sorry."

What a reminder to me that I/you can have all the plans we want, but they do not guarantee a good fit.

For the World Weary, when facing dark times, times that do not fit what was planned, this is tough. What makes this so difficult for high achievers is that we have banked our lives on striving; on the proposition that if only we "try harder" then somehow we will be magically protected from catastrophe. Not that we do this consciously, but we do unconsciously organize our lives along these concepts. We fall into the illusion, like Odysseus, that we can control the Fates. The process of recovery is rigorous. The point is that who you are beneath your striving holds great worth *if you stop being so hard on yourself* and enjoy what's before you more. Persevere in the direction of your heart's delight.

Let go of what drains you. Since it is futile to be who you aren't, what if you eased into what inspires you, restores your energy, and puts a smile on your lips? Persevere without strain.

One of my favorite Jungian analyst colleagues, Edward Edinger shared with me:

> . . . with perseverance, light is born from the darkness. One meets the "Immortal One" who sounds and heals, who casts down and raises up, who makes small and large—in a word the One who makes one whole.

Keep in mind, however, that perseverance has nothing to do with striving, pushing, racing, or trying, like those drivers on the road who race in and out of other vehicles, going way above the speed limit. It is, rather, a matter of clear intention (from heart rather than head) to focus like the eye of the tiger and remain "steady as you go" with lots of laughter and relaxation. Only your "not good enough" attitude will resist, because it is accustomed to mistrusting your deepest being. Our body is attuned to this.

The next time you start clenching your jaw or white-knuckling it again, remember that this old habit will only get you lost. When you tense up, you are not trusting your heart's authentic longing, which is where your joy lives. Writer John Eldridge put it beautifully when he said, "When we lose the heart's longing, its secret life, we are lost."

Want your life back? Then give your whole heart to your secret longing and live it up! The clue for how to do this just might be in noticing "man's best friend." For more on this, turn the page.

CHAPTER 48

The Way of the Dog:
What Would Rosie Do?

When all else fails in establishing a loving relationship with little ol' you, you might do well to consider 'The Way of the Dog.' Dog Tao is simple. Pure love, period. Our Wheaton terrier, Rosie Bell, who died fourteen years ago, taught us much of what we know about the audacity of love. In many ways, Rosie contributed to laying this cornerstone in our family's heart. No matter what you might do (have too little dog food, tire from throwing her toy, etc.) or fail to do (come back home earlier, be skimpy on the petting, forget to change her water), Rosie loved you like there was no tomorrow. She loved your bad mood into a good one. Her greetings were so heart-warming because all you needed to do was come around the corner and she acted as you were her long lost best friend, home at last! When we had to put her down, her last movement was to lick my nose.

So, when you are not having a heart for your heart, ask yourself, "What would Rosie do?" Follow The Way of the Dog. You'll be the happier for it, I promise.

What will bring you back into a more loving relationship with who you really are is this level of unconditional self-compassion and self-regard. Don't worry, it is not narcissistic! (There is such a thing as healthy narcissism, you know. It means developing healthy boundaries, even with yourself.) When you greet whatever you believe is unacceptable in yourself (or others) with warmth and presence, you'll feel better. You will reconnect with what makes you glad to be alive.

Prescription

Now, then, take yourself to the next prescription. Which pet has taught you about connection? Which young child has demonstrated a joy for life? How? Here's a space for you to remember your own "Master Teachers."

Let me give you an example: I remember my daughter Brandy, who, at three years old, would run into our bedroom and over to the window and say, "Oh boy, Mama, it's another brand new beautiful day!"

I remember my granddaughter, Talia's smile when she sees me; her vulnerable, whole-hearted outreach without pretense.

Notes to Remember

I remember:

_____

_____

I remember:

_____

_____

I remember:

_____

_____

I remember:

_____

_____

I now realize what I need to do more is:

_____

_____

SECTION FOUR

The Fourth Cornerstone: Bringing the Blueprint to Life

Courage is the commitment to begin without any guaranteeof success.

Anonymous

CHAPTER 49

Surrendering to Joy

The Law of Creation

Living our best heart-led life sooner or later leads us to face a profound question: why are you here? What within you yearns to serve? Here's a hint. What brings you to life? What desire, what passion, fans your creative spark? Whatever is yours becomes your fourth cornerstone to building a better, heart-led life, but this is not a slam dunk.

Putting the fourth cornerstone in place is tricky. It requires more patience than we think we have. Ordinarily, we go to the logical mind for a speedy plan. This never produces a heart-centered inspiration. Consider the architect. He/she cannot slap something together on a blueprint without considering the specifics of the ground, otherwise the building will neither be special nor stable.

Creating a better life requires researching our own best solid ground. This means going to the core of who we really are. Unfortunately, we have concluded that who we really are is not acceptable. OK, so how do we get there? How do we discover what is underneath all the costumes we've been wearing in order to please others?

The answer is found through depth work via meditation, exploring dreams, synchronicities, body awareness, time in nature, creative expression and whatever brings peace to the troubled mind. Doing so, brings us into alignment with what is called the natural Law of Creation. This Law tells us that all creation requires a certain process, one that begins with the end point in mind. The ego wants to believe it is in charge of the endpoint. But the most satisfying endpoint begins with inspiration! However, my friend, the problem is that the ego is in a hurry and hurry doesn't produce what is most satisfying. Ask any architect!

So you see, the most gratifying procedure comes from connecting with our innate inner wisdom and herein lies the problem: our world is always in a rush. To connect with what is most meaningful requires time, patience, and stillness. Doing so joins us with the deepest principles of gratifying creation. This is what is meant by the Law of Creation: aligning with design that is beyond what the logical brain believes possible. That said, with whatever choices are laid out before us, we can learn over time to leap into the unknown —but this is scary! If we are willing to enter the heart's guidance, with its wee small voice, this puts us into harmony with that which is greater than ourselves. These choices, more than anything else, will usher in an expanded experience of the joy which comes from trusting the process of our own path. Doing so means following the Law of Creation.

Now, it is one thing to dare vulnerability and connection when things are going beautifully in your life, and quite another to be self-compassionate when the stormy waters threaten you at sea. Just yesterday, a highly successful 'mover and shaker' type of woman came to see me and said, "I'm outgoing and joyful when I've got results. But there's another 'me' who I don't like when I get withdrawn and too quiet."

When I asked when the latter shows up, she replied, "Like now, in these terrible times. I usually try to stay busy, so I don't have to feel what's coming to the surface."

What she does not understand is that the Law of Creation is responding to her reaction.

She is not alone. When we get uncomfortable, most of us 'run to the hills' in some way (drinking, shopping, smoking, workaholism, gossip, drugging, or binging and purging, for example).

Name your excess of choice. The problem with this, however, is that the more we 'numb out' to what is arising, the more we lose our way. When this happens, we have not yet found the secret for how to employ the Law of Creation on our own behalf.

Here's a small example. I have never had what's called a sweet tooth, nor the craving for a snack after 8:00 p.m. Despite this, for the past few years, I have seemed to develop one. Finally, it dawned on me that this behavioral shift coincides with my husband's moving to an assisted living place for the perpetual care a Parkinson's sufferer requires. Bingo! The aforementioned cravings were to fill the invisible hole I felt in his absence. It helps to know the catalyst for such behaviors that sabotage what we intend. By the way, since this was made clear to me there have been no late cravings. Go figure.

What we forget is that nothing new breaks forth without first experiencing frustration, chaos, darkness, and a mess. In Genesis and its creation story (as well as other cross-cultural creation myths explaining how we came to be), you may recall that before the Earth and human life evolved, there was darkness and then "brooding waters." Symbolically, this is a metaphorical reference to the psyche's (Soul's) churning. Out of the dark and unknown depths, something is forming. Since neither you, nor I, know precisely what aspect is seeking life, we get tense. We try to plug the hole. We use whatever we use as our 'habitual fix,' be it late night candy, popcorn, internet shopping, or whatever.

This never works long-term. Like everything else in Creation, we are here to evolve, like the little acorn before it becomes a mighty oak.

The oak, like our lives, requires certain nurturing conditions. For the acorn seed, this means it must get cold before it can germinate and grow. For us, the cold might be the experience of trauma, grief, or loss. Like the little acorn, we must get clear about what conditions we require to develop. But in order to develop, we have got to be better at 'letting go,' and 'letting it be,' even when 'it' is temporary turbulence. "Why?" you may ask. Simply put, your successful relationship to your world requires you to grow. Your growth requires you to expand your way of seeing your relationship to the Law of Creation.

So often, when the topic of Creation comes up, we think of it as a historical event. Whether you are a "Creationist" or an "Evolution-ist" does not matter here. What does matter is that you are willing to expand your frame. Otherwise, it will not be possible to lay the fourth cornerstone prerequisite for getting more out of life.

Prescription

Let me ask you a question. Have you ever had a creative urge to just 'jump out of the box' and create something in your life that, even thinking about it, makes you incredibly happy, even if it might have seemed completely unreasonable or nuts to others? How far did you get in bringing your idea into concrete form? What made you hesitate? How and why did you abandon your creative new dream?

_____

_____

_____

If it were possible to create your heart's desire right now, what would you build? If time and money were not issues, what would you create? Take a moment, and using your creative imagination, as vividly as possible, pretend your dream has come about. What are you experiencing? Feeling? Fill out the following.

_____

_____

_____

_____

Now let's get honest. If you were to sabotage this heart's desire, this yearning for greater aliveness, what story would you tell yourself, like you have before?

_____

_____

_____

How would you feel if you denied yourself this new life?

_____

_____

_____

Without doing what is required, it is not possible to get a better working understanding of the Law of Creation for what's ahead.

Remember, implanted in every living thing is the urge for growth. If sufficient space, nurturing, and safety aren't present, what is meant to be gets stunted. Consider the acorn that never becomes the oak.

Ongoing Creation

Here's the truth: you couldn't stop creating if you wanted to, because you are part of an ongoing Creation. We might not like what we are creating at all times, but it is our nature to create, nonetheless. Think about it: creative Life Substance is constantly flowing through you, animating each breath, each expression, even if it's simply a doodle. You can't help yourself because this is your birthright. This Source of Life is keeping you alive. You can use it to defeat you, or to advance your dreams.

The only question is: how do you wish to use this capacity to create? For a Greater Good in your life, or to defeat a Greater Good? You can resist the power of this Greater Life if you want, but nature always wins. Best to go with the flow, best to go with the river in the direction it's moving. What would this look like in that area of your life that you have been currently resisting, but which needs facing? Describe the change you've been resisting which needs your attention. What change is it time to make?

_____

_____

_____

We do best when we stop fighting life. It is what it is: Creation unfolding, moving in the direction of growth that is ultimately best for us, even if it's inconvenient and makes us shed what we don't feel ready to shed. Even if it takes a while to "connect the dots."

An illustration

When I was growing up, one of my favorite things to do was to share mysteries with my father, first the ones I heard on the radio, and later those I saw on film and television. When my children were born, the tradition continued.

Eventually, my daughter and I grew quite fond of the Agatha Christie series called *Murder, She Wrote*. The heroine of the series, Jessica Fletcher, lived in a quaint village called Cabot Cove, where she wrote murder mysteries. I'm not sure which we liked more: the stories, the setting, or the typewriter she used. We loved them all, fantasizing about what it would be like to live in Cabot Cove. We had many conversations about this fantasy . . . or was it?

Some years later, in 2003, we came back to Washington state and as we went through a lazy little town on Bainbridge Island, we mused, "Hey, this is like Cabot Cove." Eventually, in 2003, a few weeks after we bought a home in Kirkland, we took a break from unpacking boxes and hopped a ferry to Bainbridge. On our travels, we came upon an open house and told the realtor we weren't looking but were curious. She asked us what we thought her listed property might need? To which I replied, "Nothing. It's lovely. Well, maybe if it were on the water!"

The woman got very animated and urged us to see a property on the south end of the island, recently converted from Army barracks. Both from Army families, my husband and I thought this was very funny, so we went there to see it. It was an amazing property, with a 220 degree view of Puget Sound, the Cascade Mountains, Mount Rainier, and Olympic National Park. But we had just bought a home. Ah, well.

Four years later, on New Year's weekend, we each did the exercise "Pretend there's complete abundance in the Universe. Where would you most desire to be one year from today?"

My guy and I reflected on the question and wrote down our answers following a meditation. It was that place on Bainbridge. Three weeks later, we went for another ferry ride. Long story short, the place was, unbeknownst to us, on the market. Two months later, the offer closed, and we had our own getaway place. The owner had dropped his asking price by $100K because I asked for him to let us know the lowest price he would accept.

Lesson learned: dare to ask for what you want to create. (You just never know.)

One day in 2007, while sitting at my writing desk in front of the water on Bainbridge, I looked out onto Puget Sound and saw two heron, geese, and one Bald Eagle circling overhead. When a flock of seagulls, flying no more than six feet beyond my window (we were in the penthouse) went by, I realized I was in my own form of Cabot Cove, writing what I liked best: the mystery of human lives unfolding.

By 2010, we knew at a Soul level that we wanted to live full-time on Bainbridge Island, even though it would be highly inconvenient for work. The challenge was that our place on the island was too small for day-to-day living, and we would need to sell it in the worst economy since the Great Depression. It sold within one week, the first offer made seventy-two hours after it was put on the market. The next challenge we had to face was our sudden grief at the loss of our beloved vacation home, and figuring out how we would find a place that we could afford; a place that was equally peaceful, beautiful, and uplifting. A place we could share with others who wanted to live more freely, creatively, and inspirationally. We made a list outlining what we wanted: water, mature trees, a Zen garden, covered porch, master bedroom on the main floor, studio, den, and was in harmony with nature, and then we went to bed. Ten hours later, on the way to the gym, we took a new road and found the house with everything on the list. Twenty-four hours later, the owners signed our offer. This is one demonstration of collaborating with the Law of Creation.

The fact is that you are here to bring forward your own beautiful creative genius into concrete expression. Remember, yours does not have to be a big deal as a new house. What would it be worth to you to actually bring your heart's delight to life, making it tangible? Look around you. There is not one single thing in your atmosphere which did not begin with an invisible idea. So, trust yourself and answer the question from the last exercise once again: what would it be like to bring your heart's delight into concrete form? Include the details.

_____

_____

_____

_____

While you were answering these questions, I looked around my master bedroom and smiled. Once, when I was in the studio, I pondered what it might be like to paint our bedroom in our favorite color? What would it be like to go to bed at night and awaken in the morning to that color? Fortunately, Ed's favorite color, periwinkle blue, is also mine. We plunged in and redid our bedroom in periwinkle blue and white. We both loved it. That was almost twenty years ago, and regardless of where we've lived, you can easily guess the color of our bedroom. Yes, maybe adopting a new paint color seems like small potatoes. It is not. Think of these little acted-upon inspirations as training wheels for living a heart-led life.

I can tell you that I have known many such experiences, and what's helped create them most has been deepening my relationship with the Law of Creation. My intention here is to provide the principles, structure, and encouragement to do just this. Your relationship with The Law of Creation is an entire life-shifter if you say yes. Use it consistently over the next six weeks, recording your findings, and you will be amazed at the shift in your relationship to the Law of Creation! Timing is everything! Why do you suppose this issue is vital for you today? Be specific.

If I don't improve my relationship to creating a more wholehearted life, the price will be:

_____

_____

_____

If I do improve my relationship to creating a more joyful life, the benefits would be:

_____

_____

_____

You've heard the statement "There are no accidents," right? Why do you imagine this subject is coming up for you today? Where are you needing more faith in your creative process? Listen, my friend: what on Earth would make you think that your own creative inspirations are just a fluke? Do you ever wonder about why it is that some folks take their creative inspiration and run with it, while yours seem to come and go without much follow-through? What makes us go from moments of feeling all fired up to faltering? We will explore this together when you turn the page.

We must have a measure of beauty in our lives proportionate to our affliction . . .

John Eldridge

CHAPTER 50

The Case of the Hula Hoop

Late one night, when I was a young girl, I awoke to the muffled sounds of my parents discussing something downstairs at the kitchen table. It was 2:00 a.m. As this was highly unusual, I crept out of bed and listened from the stairs. Finally, unable to make out what was happening, I took courage by the hand, walked into the kitchen in my flannel nightie, and asked, "What's going on?"

They looked at each other and decided to lay the situation out for me. (This was odd in itself! Ours was not what was called a child-centered home.) Anyway, my father told me he had until 6:00 a.m. Pacific time to respond to an offer he had received the day before from a new toy manufacturer in New York, to become the exclusive distributor of the invention. "What is it?" I asked.

"This is strange," said my father, "it's a toy your mother and I saw other kids having, but the stick that you'd guide down the street is not part of this toy. What use can it be?"

By 9:00 a.m. Eastern time, my father declined the offer. The "toy" became the hula hoop, an invention that today, some sixty years later, is still found in toy stores and gyms internationally.

Lesson learned: when we resist the Law of Creation by thinking "inside the box," we close important (and, potentially lucrative) doors.

William James tells us:

. . . . The great revolution in our generation is the discovery that human beings, by changing the inner attitudes of their minds, can change the outer aspects of their lives.

All I know is that every single time I see a hula hoop, I am reminded that keeping our thinking and assumptions in too small a box inevitably produces a limited result.

The experience of the Self is always a defeat for the ego.

C.G. Jung

Living in the Gap

One of my favorite teachers of the late nineteenth, early twentieth century, a healer by the name of Emma Curtis Hopkins, puts it this way: "You will notice that the instant you acknowledge that there is Good for you which you ought to have, the thought arises within your mind that you do not have the Good that belongs to you. You feel that your Good is *absent from you.*"

The fact is that we know this experience, don't we? Too much of the time, we live in this gap. You might identify what you want, but almost instantaneously, there's this niggling little voice Buddhists call the "monkey mind,'" and we shrinks refer to as "the ego." Whatever you want to call it, it doesn't matter. What is important is the recognition that, in a nanosecond, a second-guessing chatter goes off in our heads which negates having our dreams come true. We have a nasty way of coming down hard on ourselves and turning our focus to the apparent obstacles. No wonder our journey home to who we really are takes longer than we would like. We invalidate our right to create what is in our heart to create. We miss the secret that *it is in our nature to create* more joy, beauty, wisdom, and solutions.

The disparity between where we are and where we want to be begins to cause mistrust. We begin wondering to ourselves, "How do I get from the old structured way I have lived, to the new restructured version? Will I ever get there? This will never happen for me!"

For most of us, the excavation to get down to our natural roots is just too much. The problem is that *without a commitment to excavate those roots, find the resulting liberation that comes from casting out what's not needed anymore (like those old houses that are falling apart and dirty diapers), we simply cannot create reinvention.*

It's no big surprise, then, that if you want to get more out of life, you've got to come into a more harmonious relationship with the Law of Creation, and this means addressing the cornerstone on which the Law of Creation rests: true surrender. This means surrender in all its forms and stages: excavation to remove the junk and retrieve what needs cherishing, followed by that fresh air experience of liberation. Your foundation must be built on solid, firm ground, and ultimately, the reinvention or framing and building of who we really are at present, both in private and public. Sorry, Charlie, but it's true. You cannot begin manifesting a juicier life without truly surrendering your old game plan and overcoming your mistrust of spontaneity.

Prescription

Describe your or your family's missed opportunities:

_____

_____

_____

_____

Describe your lesson learned:

_____

_____

_____

_____

What lesson do you need to take to heart and learn today?

_____

_____

_____

_____

What secret are you uncovering about what's possible for you that you've imagined up to now?

_____

_____

_____

_____

CHAPTER 51

The Little Planner

L et me illustrate how laying the fourth cornerstone requires true surrender.

It means awakening to what stops us short of creating and living out our heart's desire. And this, my friend, especially if you are a world weary, involves facing "the little planner."

Our 'little planner' has a way of living in the future; preparing long to-do lists before there is space to live spontaneously in the present.

The following process helped me to understand what was in my way from fully embracing all that I could be and shows you what you can do to become better and better partners with the Law of Creation. (Which, by the way, no one had put together for me until this event.) At the time, I was feeling all the stress that goes along with cramming too many clients into sessions the week before I was to leave for Asia to lead one of the retreats I do called "The Listening Heart." There just didn't seem to be enough time as I darted here and there, scooping up notes and references in every spare minute, generally driving myself crazy. The clock was ticking and my insomnia was growing. My chest felt tighter and tighter. What to do? I felt like the rabbit in *Alice in Wonderland*, running around my own self-created hamster wheel, chanting "I'm late! I'm late . . . for a very important date. No time to say "hello," goodbye, I'm late! I'm late! I'm late!"

Ever been there? I was sucked into that race with the clock like planes in a San Francisco fog. There was no way to move. The stress reached such a crescendo that I did what I always do at times like these, at least for the past fifty-two years, particularly, since my son was killed.

Getting Off the Hamster Wheel

I hauled myself up by the bootstraps and got off the hamster wheel long enough to meditate. I began to ask the question, "What was this racing really about?"

The answer came swiftly. It shocked me. Underneath my long-standing achieving-producing act was the truth: I was terrified of going to Taipei empty-handed, without a pre-developed script. There was this belief I had been holding that I needed props, all the bells and whistles, to do my best. But the reality was that all this stuff was completely in my way.

I smelled a rat! Beneath the fear of being with people I had never met without a tightly-controlled schtick was the realization that I would feel too vulnerable. Just like them, I'd be clueless about what would happen next, and I was their leader. Not good! Here's the kicker: people who know me would swear that I am a champ at spontaneity. One longtime friend said that if you look up the word in the dictionary, you'll see my picture right next to it. But in this instance, I was bringing truly new material to the event, and I had fallen into the old trap of thinking the source of it was outside myself.

It was at that precise moment that the joke hit me. My fear was exactly what the participants must be feeling! They were coming in trust. Most of them did not know me. No marketing material could describe the mysterious event. People who had worked with me told others, "You just have to be there."

So, people were coming to a place they'd never been, with a leader they had not met, to do what they did not know, for a price most could not afford, and they were doing so anyway.

What about me? Suddenly it dawned on me that we needed to be in the question mark together. Why? Very simply, because we'd all traveled our own path to arrive where we were together: a place on the Edge that separated the space between our history and the present moment. No one knew what lay ahead; we were in the Mystery and pretending that we weren't. It was not only the Edge that was creating anxiety, but it was also the fact that we pretended we weren't dealing with the Mystery. We all like to pretend we are in control! We aren't.

The funny thing was that this is what I've always loved the absolute most in working with groups: connecting moment to moment with Life's Mystery and strategizing how best to maximize the transforming strengths that would come out of the process together. What I had never realized before that moment was that my practice of serious preparation before keynotes, seminars, and retreats, for over thirty-five years by then, had really been a way of keeping myself occupied sufficiently beforehand so as not to feel the angst of that old fear of creating from the unknown. Excessive preparation was just a way I had learned to organize around my fear.

Whereas preparation builds skill sets and mastery, excessive preparation kills new life by over-filling the space that new life requires. My little planner was in overkill. Overplanning leads not to freedom but to imprisonment by fear. When I made a sketch of Little Planner, she was a serious little girl with an unending roll of paper on which she was ticking off my chores. I, on the other hand, looked like a person on a cross, being crucified by rules, regulations, and fear.

The good news, as author Malcolm Gladwell pointed out a number of years later in *Outliers*, is that those who master their trade have put in over 10,000 hours, which is about five years, full-time, until they get to mastery. By then, I'd logged in seven times that amount of time in what I do, so I know the drill and can easily freelance. That's the liberating thing about having loads of practice doing what you love. But practice, my friend, is not the same thing as excessive pre-planning, otherwise known as over-planning.

You see, I woke up to what is true: it wasn't true that I couldn't figure out what to do on the spot. That's my forte. I can teach people how to do that. I just needed to keep myself occupied before I stood on uncharted territory and just dive in. In an instant, I was liberated! I realized the real purpose of my work and why this brings me such joy. This kind of joy is a big hint that you are on the trail of your own heart-led living.

Excessive preparation kills new life.

Cara Barker

Since then, sometimes I slip back into that old groove, but when I do, I catch myself faster and stop, look, and re-choose how I want to enter the prep period. I use the time beforehand in far more pleasant ways, mostly moving in whatever direction speaks to my heart. Inevitably it turns out to be the very experience I need to draw upon in teaching practices people most want to learn in that setting. But you never know what that will be until the moment arrives, and with it, your surrender to The Law of Creation: what you think about, you bring about.

What gets in the way of our right to joy and liberation is that Little Planner. Since I found my own, every single person I have worked with who really wants to create a life that's free has been able to recognize their own little planner. Better yet, we are learning how to enlist the little planner in a much more pleasant and life-renewing adventure. Awakening is everything! We are not talking politics here; rather, we are talking about waking up.

Go with the flow

If you are an achieving-producing type, and you notice your Little Planner gets activated, please remember this is a signal that working harder is the very opposite of the thing you need to be doing. Little Planner signals you are needing to take a creative break, breathe in, breathe out, and give it a rest before you can resume along a more pleasing and productive direction. Little Planner is terrified of letting down someone you value, and so is a particularly important messenger that you are needing to call back your Spirit and your life.

In her book, *Lessons in Living*, Susan L. Taylor, puts it this way:

No matter what we may think, or feel, regardless of appearances, life is always on our side, always offering us the experiences we need to make changes and grow. Feeling myself losing myself rerouted me. It prompted me to pursue balance as a goal in my life.

When we fail to do as Susan suggests, we slip into resentment/ victimizations coming from a failure in self-care. It is less a matter of lack of love for the other, and more an issue of your well going dry for your Soul. But not only that. The fact is that your Little Planner will drive you into working harder and harder. This only gets in the way of partnership with the Law of Creation.

Prescription

It's time to pause, breathe, reflect, and take a break. Consider the last time you were overworking, trying too hard, tense, or trying to please. Describe:

_____

_____

_____

Now, using your creative imagination, doodle a cartoon figure that illustrates your Little Planner, in the following space.

What is your cartoon Little Planner saying to you?

_____

_____

_____

Now, using your creative imagination, tell your Little Planner what you need most:

_____

_____

_____

CHAPTER 52

Placing Your Order

Coming home to greater self-love, to the secret of getting more out of life, is done by adjusting your relationship with the Law of Creation. How do you do this?

Let's use a metaphor. Last Sunday, my sister-friend Jane and I wanted to get a bite to eat. We decided Mexican food would be good. We stopped at an available outside table on what was an amazingly sunny autumn day.

Imagine yourself sitting in a restaurant, your mouth watering for a fresh Caesar salad, gazpacho soup, and char-grilled Pacific Northwest halibut. The server takes out her pad of paper and asks you what you want. You say, "Bring me food."

She returns with a wilted salad, liver and onions, which you hate, and boiled turnips, which have always made you feel like throwing up. You object. It's not what you wanted, right? However, she brought her response to the order you placed. If you aren't getting what you want, reconsider the order you are placing, especially what you are asking for unconsciously.

For instance, I know women, and you probably do, too, who say, "I'd love to find a partner. But there are no good men left out there!"

What do they get? "No good men!" This is the order they have placed, and the Law of Creation responds impersonally, without judgment, in accord with your belief, or "order." All I know is that I've had two great husbands (not at the same time), and I met each one directly after I wrote down what I wanted and placed my order. I met my first husband within two weeks of writing down my request, and my second, within one week. Although no one advised me to do this, at the time, what I knew was that the other ways of meeting men, that whole rat race, seemed a waste of energy. Once I exited from the struggle, life opened up and I will always be grateful.

You see, my dear, the Universe has your back to help you construct a better life. First, however, you've got to trust you are part of something much bigger, much more powerful, much more imaginative than your little lonesome, if you are willing to give this bigger life a chance. Quit trying so hard. Your freedom requires your cooperation. Being a "human doing" is not only unattractive, but it repels help and hinders magical breakthroughs.

I realize that, to your human-doing-ness's perspective, your great suspicion is probably arising about now. Little Planner lives by the mantra, "If it's to be it's up to me." The problem is that it's not true. Freedom insists on cooperation. If you want to create more joy, let Creative Intelligence have its way with you. Let it give you a hand. Remember that true story at the beginning of this book? Those construction workers were faced with digging down to a solid foundation level on which to frame and build what had been imagined. They were not alone in building. Neither are we. What stops us? We turn to often to others for what we should do, rather than where the focus needs to be.

How, you ask? By giving yourself to yourself before you give yourself away.

Maybe for you, this means meditation, progressive relaxation, candles, favorite passages, a fifteen minute walk by the lake in the in the desert, or through the forest, park, or zoo. It could also be swinging a golf club or tennis racket or going for a hike with your dog. Just do whatever brings you to Stillness. To do so is not malignant narcissism. Recall when I mentioned healthy narcissism a short time ago. Part of that healthy narcissism means building better boundaries. Just remember that 'no' is a complete sentence. This can be beyond challenging for those of us who have been giving ourselves away when our energy reserves are shot.

I often think of the famous C.S. Lewis quote: "Praying doesn't change God. It changes me."

Well, doing this process doesn't change the Law of Creation. It changes your relationship with it so that you can work in greater harmony with your Greater Good as you unfold. This is your Edge: shifting away from working too hard, shifting away from self-criticism and stress to self-care. If you refuse, you stay stuck.

Jiddu Krishnamurti used these words to say it better than I:

> We think the problem is out there, in society. The problem is not out there. The problem is really inward and we are not willing to face it.

Prescription

Focus on an area of your life where you would like to make improvement. Record your order here, giving particular attention to details:

_____

_____

_____

_____

What self-compassionate step do you need to take next?

_____

_____

_____

_____

CHAPTER 53

Getting Out of Your Head Without Parking Your Brain at the Door

Using the Law of Creation for better results won't come from more theories or intellectualizing, but rather from shifting your very state of mind toward a Greater Good than you've ever imagined, toward thoughts you've never dared to have, or taken seriously, by placing orders that have either been too small or lackluster for what is in your heart. Let me repeat these three steps:

1. Shift your thinking toward your Greater Good.

2. Shift toward bigger possibilities.

3. Place better, more joy-based orders.

Now, the fourth:

4. Let go of attachments to how your intentions will show up. The Universe responds best when you remain open.

This process is not something someone reads or hears. It's something witnessed and incorporated into the best you, which becomes the greater you. So, you see, your very core is nudging you to grow and to shed another layer so it can use you as one of Its infinite outlets to bring about something much more creative and inspiring in your life, right here, right now. Your life is not just about you. Your life is an aspect of the One Life, of which we are each a part; a life that is the Divine's life. Whether it's comfortable or not, we are all here to play a part in something more beautiful, more abundant, and more meaningful than any of us can imagine.

So, place a more delicious order and get specific! Now, I'm not saying that doing so means you run around, repeating hollow affirmation statements scribbled on 3x5 index cards over and over like a robot. You do not place your order like a zombie. What you have to do is take the time and space to lay fallow for a while, like the earth between crops, preparing the soil, cultivating the atmosphere for the seed of a sincere feeling to take root and grow over time. While we might like instant results, as any new mama knows, instant rice does not offer the same nourishment as the traditional ways of making rice. You can't rush the process and expect to get the best outcome. One helpful reference is a nifty little book called *The Gift of a Year* by Myra Kirshenbaum. Check it out for additional ideas and structure.

Growing Trust

You've got to get better at trusting the process of discovering what your heart really wants.

you've got to get better at forgiving yourself for wrong choices. We all make them. You've got to start cultivating a healthy respect for the one in the mirror and trust that your present condition, and you, yourself, are not a mistake. Rather, you are an instrument for Life to shine through with greater light, clarity, creativity, wisdom, and Love than ever before, through your present situation. Whatever Edge you are facing that's unexpected, it's the exact one that you need. If Jesus did not face the garden of his doubt and suffering on Good Friday, Easter could not have come. If his mother did not lose her son, she would not have known that Life goes on. If Buddha or Saint Francis did not have issues with their fathers, their ways of modeling awakening would not have emerged. If Mary Cassatt had not loved simple scenes of mothers and children, and defied the patriarchal rules of what makes a painting important, the world of impressionism would be grieving. The same holds true for Frida Kahlo. The examples go on and on.

Discoveries from the Heart

After losing her kidnapped and murdered child, and going on to grow through it, Anne Morrow Lindberg placed her order for an expanding life.

She wrote:

When we start at the center of ourselves, we discover something worthwhile, extending toward the periphery of the circle. We find again some of the joy in the now, some of the peace in the here. Some of the love in the me and the thee which go to make up the Kingdom of heaven on earth.

It's easy to draw the conclusion that arriving at such a relationship with the Law of Creation is easier for others than it is for you. Not so.

She goes on to write:

The sea does not reward those who are too anxious, too greedy, or too impatient. To dig for treasures shows not only impatience and greed, but lack of faith. Patience, patience, patience is what the sea teaches. Patience and faith. One should lie empty, open, choiceless as a beach—waiting for a gift from the sea.

Regarding patience, if you've ever had a dog or cat, you've seen patience at work: patience like Rosie (described earlier) had in digging away to extract a flea, or your pet's antics, doing whatever they do to get back into life's flow. Not unlike our little kitten Chelsey, who would press her black furry paw underneath the door to my consulting room when she wanted to be included and cuddled. Neither our animals nor we need to intellectualize the "fleas" away. We need to trust and follow the wisdom of our instincts.

The Eternal Struggle for Patience

Great mythological stories endure through the centuries because they are as sound today for our evolution as they were when they were written and tend to remind us of this ongoing struggle to learn patience. In the tale of *Psyche and Amour*, Psyche needed to accomplish certain tasks to liberate her into the next round of her evolution (sorting, gathering, patience, secured boundaries). These are your tasks, and each of ours who wish to develop an authentic relationship with feelings, heart wisdom, and our own bodies. Their mystery is instrumental to really relating to others, beginning with yourself, which is why meditation is so helpful, be it sitting on a cushion in lotus position or doing engaged meditation.

People around you will be glad you took the time to get out of your busy head for a while and into your centered heart. Likewise, they will notice when you don't. I recall such a time when my daughter, Brandy, was three years old. One day she turned to me and said, "Mommy, did you 'mekikate' (meaning meditate) today? I think you should!"

Busted. She was right. Rushing, I had failed to do my practice and had gotten cranky. Back to the pillow for me. We were both happier for the relief!

My own practice works best when I do a combination of sitting meditation coupled with engaged, where I draw the central focus that comes, not for artistic merit, but as a means of honoring what is within me that's calling for attention. It has been especially helpful during my roughest times.

I'm not alone. For the great Swiss psychiatrist, Carl Jung, the practice of expressing imagery from his depths illuminated his way during his darkest night. By honoring his personal inner calling, he helped untold thousands around the world. Here's what he recorded in the famous *Red Book*, his private journal which was not released until 2010:

> . . . . I wanted to throw everything away and return to the light of the day. But the Spirit stopped me and forced me back into myself.

The irony is that it can seem like those periods of your toughest storms have no bearing on what you want to create. *But it is these most deeply human experiences that have the power to drive you to face yourself as never before.* And these same events that forge your character and the reassurance you give to others through the example of how you live your life. I realize it's not much consolation, but don't kid yourself: the most challenging times are your alchemical opportunity to 'turn lead into gold.' We must realize we've been asleep before we awaken. Tough times are not the end, they are the beginning of improvement, if you are willing to pay the dues. Some people pay bigger fees than others. Significant rebirth exacts significant sacrifice.

Just ask the ancestors. They paid quite the price tag to do what they did, in accordance with their own level of understanding. Rarely had an ancestor heard of the Law of Creation, although it was at work in their lives, just as it now is through yours. But they knew a great deal about tough times.

"Be Still" Original painting (in color) by Cara Barker, 1995

During the most trying times, the DNA of humankind has called us to return within, to enter the stillness, and prepare the way for the wee small voice in the darkness.

I don't know how long we stood gazing at the new tree 'hatching' from the old stump. All I know is that it seemed to me God was speaking eloquently once again about rebirth. . . .

A simple message about how life comes out of death and healing comes out of scars and wounds. The message said that rebuilding can happen after leveling . . . that hope is bigger than despair.

Sue Monk Kidd

CHAPTER 54

Practicing the Law of Creation During Toughest Times

D o you ever wonder why so many good folks get slammed with the tough breaks? So often, when sitting with the people most dear to my heart, I have been confounded by why it is that such profound suffering has come to the door of someone so generous, inspiring, and awake? Why is it that the "greats" are so often challenged with the worst tragedies? These very people respond in such remarkably self-aware ways that by sheer example, they give the gift of a consciously-lived life, which ends up assisting others by sheer modeling. This doesn't mean they haven't struggled. Quite the opposite.

That said, our hope is reignited by the creatively courageous who do not turn away from life's demands but use them as compost for working with the Law of Creation, whether they call it this or not, to connect with life more deeply to co-create. They have sufficient awareness to work creatively with what comes, whatever that may be.

When the Difficult Comes, You Never Know Who's Watching

Some sixteen years after my son's funeral, I was dumbstruck by a woman who told me that a number of kids who came to the wake and funeral reported that they had been helped by how we dealt with our loss. Apparently, this was their first exposure to death, and the way the young people were welcomed helped them to not be as frightened in the years to come. You never know who's watching. At that time, I was simply doing the best I could to follow my instincts, take one step at a time, and be present. The furthest thing from my mind was making an impression. It has been said that your greatest gifts given are the miracles of which you are unaware.

Prescription

Describe two people who have most deeply inspired you and why.

_____

_____

_____

_____

CHAPTER 55

Entanglement

We can only begin to understand and appreciate the Law of Creation when we're willing to let go the Newtonian belief in separation. As science is demonstrating, even at the sub-atomic, molecular level, we are what they call "entangled." What affects one part affects the whole. What affects you affects me. We are more than connected as inter-related beings; we are indelibly intertwined with Creation, itself. We are inextricably linked with one another, with the Cosmos, and with all life in ways that the human mind does not comprehend.

The only time we ever know what's really going on is when the rug is pulled out and we can't find anywhere to land.

Pema Chodron

Let me give you another example of this at work. In the "Rainmaker" story, which we know is true because Richard Wilhelm, who had lived for a long time in China, recorded it. Apparently, in a certain village there was desperate suffering from severe drought. The villagers had tried everything imaginable to make the rain fall. They'd gone to their monks, who hung prayer flags, the priests who lit incense, the ministers who evoked prayers. Nothing worked. Finally, they sent a messenger off to a remote village to enlist the Rainmaker. After a long journey back, hot, dusty, and weary, the Rainmaker asked to be shown to his quarters and for a bit of food. He did not come out for four days, during which period not one raindrop fell, nor cloud appeared. On the fourth day he emerged, and the rain fell. Amazed, the villagers asked what magic he had performed? What was his secret? He replied, "None," and went on to tell them his truth. When he'd arrived, he noticed immediately that he felt "out of sorts" with the tension in the air. Thus, he retired to his own space to re-establish harmony with his own core and, therefore, Creation. The net result was "a miracle," but we have forgotten how essential it is to return to the flow in the present moment and accept the power of your relationship to Creation in this moment. The power of this secret Way cannot be overstated.

Our tasks, like the Rainmaker's, are four-fold, and each involve practice. Each step is simple. However, you must practice, because to master them, you've got to give up self- defeating tendencies, which is not easy. However, if you genuinely want to experience heart-led living, the following will assist you greatly. It's simple, but not easy! So, here they are:

1. Practice focusing your awareness.

Notice your experience. Trust what comes. Surrender to Life Substance, which is larger than you. Align with Creation. Things turn out much better this way! The Rainmaker observed his sense of discomfort. His next step was to prepare the atmosphere in which he felt free to return to inner peace. He did not skip this essential step. You cannot create improved conditions without first centering in silence.

2. Practice coming into true relations with all things.

Even the most challenging. New life will come again to the degree that you practice connecting with the bigger story of which you are a part. Find nourishment within a larger tribe. When called, the Rainmaker traveled and responded to a bigger need.

3. Practice taking only true action.

Do only that which resonates with your heart, bypassing the rest.

P.S. This means releasing the need to "multi-task." There's plenty of evidence that we don't do well at this, and we're not designed to function this way. When you experience distress, let go of your need to fix anything. This will lead you astray. Once you get real about your feelings and focus, the one next truest step will emerge. For the Rainmaker, this was when he came out of the hut.

4. Express, in your own most naturally creative way, what you discover.

Others might benefit from what you have learned. Choose whatever form most delights your heart.

Knowing that this is what's before you in the Creation department can give you a headache if your little monkey mind decides this is going to be hard. Forget hard. Stay with true. Stay with your creative imagination. Play, mess around. This is all about taking yourself out of the trying-too-hard pattern, remember?

When I catch myself getting overly ambitious, overwhelmed, or caught in what I call 'seriousity,' I like to remember this verse translated by Nyoshul Khenpo called "Om Ah Hung Bensa" from a Tibetan poem. I've probably butchered those names, but we can all relax, because working in harmony with the Law of Creation has nothing to do with striving for perfection.

Rest in natural great peace, This exhausted mind,
Beaten helplessly by karma and neurotic thoughts.
Like the relentless fury Of the pounding waves
On the infinite Sea of Samsara. Rest in natural great peace.

Nyoshul Khenpo

The Rainmaker was a champion in this, wasn't he? He rested. He trusted his need to reconnect with his own center, to give this the time it took, to trust he was a part of a bigger, ongoing Creation, and to value and express his truth simply, through his expanding role. He was willing to travel from where he had lived to new territory. He said "yes" to the new change, the new adventure, a new level of solution. Listen to what some impressive men and women have said about their findings in this area:

All stress comes about through resistance to change.

Judge Thomas Troward

You cannot solve a problem at the level of the problem.

Albert Einstein

If you try to resist your present life change, you'll only make matters worse.

This includes as we get older. No wonder Castellejo has observed that: "Countless older women escape silently down the kitchen sink along with their tears. . . ." whereas, "If the old can become creative in their own right . . . they are lost no longer."

So, no matter how many wrinkles you've got, or don't, *now* is the time to start enriching through practicing your relationship with the Law of Creation. How do you do this?

I suggest you take to heart the sage advice of Judge Thomas Troward, mentioned previously:

> . . . . the first thing in any investigation is to have some idea of what you are looking for—to have at least some notion of the general direction in which to go—just as you would not go up a tree to find fish, though you would for bird's eggs.

Let's summarize:

1. Consider your vision of the life you want to build.

If you want to travel to Bellingham, why would you take a bus, train, or automobile headed for San Francisco?

2. You cannot authentically "meet'" another unless you are most naturally yourself.

During the "caterpillar" period, the caterpillar itself moves into a chrysalis where its latest form melts before it emerges as a butterfly. Each stage is necessary. Same thing is true in human nature. Our so-called meltdowns are Nature's way of nudging our old way of identifying ourselves into something more beautiful.

3. Edges school you on the necessity of meeting life more sincerely.

Author/analyst Alice Miller, who I highly recommend to you, has made an invaluable study of the consequences of failed meetings between children and their parents, which brings about a certain falseness and related distress. The takeaway from her work is to that you must encourage your own journey by acknowledging the Truth of who you are and how you came to be. I invite you to do this on paper. Take whatever time it takes and use whatever words that tell the truth in your own way. You'll need this for what comes next. You might begin as though you were standing on the Edge of your life, looking back on your own history.

Think about it this way: you have, no doubt, noticed an increasing interest in ancestry. More and more people are exploring their roots and the secrets that have been hidden in their family tree.

An Ancestral Example

In my own case, you could say I was a "roving reporter" as a child. I felt compelled to solve the mystery of people's underlying stories. I had no idea that what prompted this behavior was a hole inside of me. Instinctively, I began chasing the tail of a missing story: the absent details in my father's family story. There seemed to be this odd sense of something he was not saying. What I did not know until researching my family tree seventeen years after his death was that my father had altered his name, birthdate, and cultural roots, unbeknownst to even my mother.

When my own paternal grandmother, who died before I met her, came to me in a dream and told me I must research her story and that of my father's people, she got my attention. This was seventeen years after my father's death. What I found changed my life. For a variety of reasons, unbeknownst to my mother and the rest of us, my dad had altered his name, birthdate, and story of origin. As an example, his family had not immigrated from England and Wales generations before, as we had been told. I was not given the name 'Lee' (Cara Lee) for my ancestor Robert E. Lee, as my father had said, because he was not actually our ancestor! The truth is that my father's family were Eastern European Jews, and my grandfather came to these shores with his wife and three children. Within two weeks after their arrival, his wife and two children died. My grandfather never recovered, and this created a very bumpy road between my father and him.

In contrast, my Finnish mother told the details of her family's story, but the physical affection was absent. The Finn side was afraid of deep feeling; another hole. Somehow, as a child I intuited missing parts of their stories which did not "flow" the way stories do when you witness the whole. Sensing the missing pieces, I blindly set out on what I call "story retrieval." What I didn't realize at the time was that my story was one of dealing with this inherited sense of absence. In my father's story, there was an absence of vital facts and feelings of profound loss. In my mother's family story, there was an absence of warmth and compassion and a sense of Soul neglect. Ultimately, I realized the imperative of coming into a good relationship with these facts if I were ever going to live whole-heartedly and as a fully alive human being.

There is something in our human nature that demands we get our story straight. There is something in our psyche which requires that we leave record of the whole. Take the journal entry of the pioneer, Algeline Ashley, as held by the Harvard Schlesinger Library in their collection of *American Women in History*: "I write on my lap with the wind rocking the wagon . . . . "

The question is why?

These are a few of the facts about my own previously unknown heritage, but there is a layer of everyone's underground story that goes just as deep. I'm asking you to discover the roots, now, of your personal process that has molded and shaped your comfort and discomfort with creative self-expression. This takes surrender, of course. Practice surrender and you will come into a much more joyful and fruitful relationship with the Law of Creation. Relax, let go, and go for imperfection.

By way of example, here's my own poem, entitled "I Was Born."

I Was Born

Reflecting Back from my own Edge:
I was born in the Church of Art, Raised in the House of Mystery,
Buried beneath layers
Of Predictability. Paint was my milk, Dance was my ground.
Performance, my bridge, Back to the Heart.
I was schooled in the College of Surprises, And damn-near
lost in the
Curriculum of Conformity, Respectability, and Approval.
My real University began
When I veered off the expected path, And sank into that vessel
Traversing uncharted waters, In absence of all
Known coordinates,
Of latitude and longitude.

Prescription

Now it's your turn. Trust whatever comes and record it without
censorship.

I was:

_____

_____

_____

_____

Let the beauty we love be what we do. There are hundreds of ways to kneel and kiss the ground.

Rumi

This is what I want you to know. You can keep turning somersaults when the "you-know-what" hits the fan, or you can surrender to becoming friends with the Law of Creation, and let it help you bring out who you truly are: a magnificent instrument of Life who's here recording your very human experience. You need not be a professional artist, author, musician, poet, dancer, or sculptor to do so. We're not talking here about your artistic achievement.

We are talking about you becoming an artist of Life. "And, what, pray tell, is that?" you might be asking.

Very simply, as an artist of Life, you are willing to come into living out the absolute best life you can, one freed up to receive what a Higher Intelligence can bring to life through yours. As the Gnostic Gospel of Saint Thomas tells us: "This is the healing that saves us." What's found runs deeper than words: it is your own true nature.

Saint Thomas puts it this way:

> If you bring forward what is within you, what is within you will save you. But, if you do not bring forward what it within you, what is within you will destroy you.

Your call.

There's good news if you choose the "bringing forward" attitude. You'll get better and better at working with the Law of Creation, over time and with practice, in the areas that mean the most to you.

This is why we women are so touched by our little gardens, or a vase of simple posies, or a homemade gift, or a beautifully prepared meal, or a little drawing, poem, sculpture, or quilt done by hand. These expressions reflect back to us how Spirit dwells in beautifully earnest expressions—a fact which eludes organized religion.

Ernest Holmes brings us to the bottom line:

"God can only do for you what He can do through you."

The Spirit of Life must feel alive.

Judge Thomas Troward

CHAPTER 56

The Power of True Surrender

Every artist worth their salt is aware that when something happens creatively, it is a surprise. It comes through a surrendered relationship with the Law of Creation. You cannot create anything worthwhile without surrendering to what's greater than you. You can learn the skills. This is important. But the skills won't take you to a magnificent work of art. For that, you've got to practice the skills, consistently, and surrender to something beyond your own vision, because it will always take an unexpected form. It's as if you are there sniffing the tail of the painting, or the phrase, or the movement or sound. You are not the whole source of what comes through, and you know it. You are grateful when something breaks through you, and finds the page, the canvas, the score of music, or the mission. It's from something beyond you, yet something of which you are a part.

Meaning, that Greater Intelligence is not somewhere "out there," but is a force pregnant with creative possibilities flowing through your veins, and all other living things, at this very moment. Just as it flowed through the teachers Jesus Christ, the Buddha, Mohammed, and others, it flows through you. For, as Ernest Holmes believed, these Masters were not the great exceptions, but, rather, the Great Examples. This means you've got to awaken your own creative ability; your own absolute freedom of action and creative power. In studio parlance, we say that an artist becomes "free of his palette." This is not art for art's sake, but art for heart's sake, and creative capacity to enjoy life at its best.

Troward said, "What we eventually attain is not what we merely wish, but what we regard as normal." Perhaps this explains Thoreau's observation that: "The mass of men live lives of quiet desperation."

When you evoke your will as your ultimate source of power, you set struggle into motion. The strain grows. The reality is that there is no power greater than your source. The only way out of your struggle is deep contemplation from your source. Let go of everything else. You've got to surrender and make a paradigm leap in the way you think. *You are not your circumstances or your conditions. They are a reflection of how you think and how you are in relatedness to the Law.*

You will find that your surrender to the Law of Creation helps you to be kinder to yourself, more allowing, and acknowledging of the fact that when you are brave enough to take on your growth, you'll have these periods when you wander, when you get a little lost, but this is just part of the process of moving forward. You'll have these times when you will find yourself a little homesick. And when you do, it's best to pack your bag, metaphorically, for whatever warms your heart, renews your spirit, and refuels your body. This is all part of your true surrender. Perhaps the biggest challenge is releasing the collective belief that you are separate; that you must 'go it alone.' You have more options than you believe right now.

Let me pause right here and remind you that developing further is facilitated by gathering with those in similar pursuit in their lives, although their way is unique. Find your tribe. For thirty-five years I offered classes and retreats focusing on meditative painting. This was a time for each participant to be their hidden self, to be completely free to respond fully to the moment from the whole of themselves. A time for spontaneous, creative reflection and expression, a form of play with our greater self, which naturally happens when we are being completely authentic.

Process painting draws you into the studio, the art of authenticity where it is the most natural thing in the world to create. Monkey mind is constantly judging, worrying, and comparing. But this is not our job. Leave striving and the weary mind behind. Here, you rekindle self-courtesy, invite yourself to lay down the burden of trying to be who you aren't and trying to impress others. Becoming courteous to your little movements and marks, and your most authentic nature. Inspiration only comes when we free ourselves up, when we lay down the burden of repeating our old patterns. Painting meditation is all about engaging with what is inside, beyond the monkey mind, and fully responding to what we meet. Expressing what's within you furthers your progress. Yes, your monkey makes the proposition scary at times. Good old monkey mind. Don't let him stop you!

Personally, I paint because I can take my time, wait for portals to open, catch them when they do, go through, discover, and embrace them. I paint as a way to come home to myself and find hidden realms, particularly when I think that what I want to express is impossible for me to express in any sort of meaningful or joyful way.

I paint when there's no one around to tell me what I can or cannot do, or that it's time to stop. I paint pictorial journals because they capture what words cannot contain, they translate what is within that needs to come forward, and some day, "heard" by my children's children's children who I've never met.

What we are in search of is the secret of getting more out of life in a continually progressive degree.

Judge Thomas Troward

Giving yourself license to express what is within you gives one means of liberation. During my Rockville period, a few months after Matt's death, while at a figure drawing class Montgomery College offered, I realized that I could no longer rush with the pack of young people and their stopwatch. I needed to tell my story first with image, and then words. It turned out to be my Way.

True surrender involves risking expression of your truest nature, not only when you are alone, but also within the heart of community that truly sees and honors who you are. This is why it is so essential to find your tribe. Once I surrendered to creating a creative community, more joy entered the picture for each of us.

Prescription

Consider some instance in your life when you experienced true surrender. Remember when you played as a child? I watched little Talia's amazement when she was a little girl as she explored everything in her atmosphere, and I remember her mama doing the same thing. I remember Brandy seeing a bird fly for the first time, raising her arms like wings, and trying to fly. Children live in a natural state of surrender. Look at their level of joy!

They live twenty-four seven "above the line." They do not concern themselves with appearances, for they trust the secret power of true surrender to the Law of Creation.

Full-on play is surrender. When you fully play, you do not know what's next. Surprise is the element that keeps the game going and keeps you on Edge. Imagine you are standing on the edge of a ring. Inside and below appears to be nothing. When you draw back from the edge, fear has you in its grip. But, when you surrender to playing in a new way, that leap of faith brings you into uncharted, lively places.

Recall such a time when you chose to dive in and you were richer for it, because you leapt with all your heart:

_____

_____

_____

_____

CHAPTER 57

The Real Question

Leaps like the one you just described are marvelous ways to practice surrender and create a more deeply satisfying life. When you lollygag you lose. This is because your sincere practice of surrender brings you home to the most vital question your Soul will ever ask you. Here's how Dr. Jung puts it:

> . . . . The decisive question for man is: Is he related to something infinite or not? That is the telling question of his life. Only if we know that the thing which truly matters is the infinite can we avoid fixing our interest upon futilities, upon all kinds of goals which are not of real importance . . . . If we understand and feel that here, in this life we already have a link with the infinite, desires and attitudes change.

Let me give you an example. This week and last after work, I've driven to another town to sit with a client who is dying of cancer. She is so brave. Just last night she said, "I've been practicing being present. When I don't run away from the Edge you describe, and I really breathe, I realize there is nothing to fear. Not that I know for sure what's in the void. I'm not sure. But I do hear and feel the silence. In this stillness, I sense this presence which tells me I'm going to be alright, whether I live through the night or die. In the stillness, I feel connection with all things, something Greater. I'm ready for what comes, either way."

Rilke puts it this way: "The Divine wants to know itself in you."

Songwriter and singer Karen Taylor-Good, through one of her songs, asks us to imagine that God's got your photo and artwork on Her refrigerator! Doesn't that make you smile? If not, reread this until it does.

Let's remember this image. Do not fall into the world's cover story that life is all about conflict, competition, defeat, or power games like those featured in the evening news. So much more is waiting for you. Let's not waste the opportunity to surrender to more possibility than ever before.

What this will take is a willingness to come to the Edge of your belief that you are separate. Challenge yourself to notice a sense of connection with all things. Dwell in the silence of this experience and cultivate gratitude for your willingness to collaborate with gratitude.

Prescription

Practice the following every day. Yes, every day for the next six weeks without fail. No guts, no glory! Yes, one more go at assisting you to build the best structure for living a more heart-led life. Begin by finding a peaceful place where you are alone. Relax. Soften your focus. Relax your eyelids. Breathe slowly in and out until you feel surrendered and centered.

NOTE: Begin by recording the following very slowly so you can hear your own voice. Or, alternatively, have someone you trust completely read it to you slowly.

Breathing slowly in and out, relaxing your body . . . letting go of any lost "Hula Hoop" opportunities in the past . . . truly surrendering to the present moment. Breathing in and out, relaxing every tiny muscle and every cell from the top of your head to the tips of your toes. Allowing your breath to remove any tension, any stress, each in-breath to restore new energy, new life.

Don't worry if you drift off to sleep. Your unconscious mind is very present, working on your behalf at all times. Dropping into that deepest place inside you, the bridge to the very Source of Life that is moving through you. This wisdom, so all-encompassing that it knows precisely what is needed in the affairs of your life to bring about a Greater Good . . . . Let go, now, of all of your many concerns, releasing all your tensions to this Greater Good, knowing that all resources are coming your way.

You do not have to know how to solve things . . . . You are not alone, but rather, a Supreme Intelligence is always with you, in this moment, and this moment, and this moment, coming to your aid, moving through your body, releasing all toxins and signs of stress, making it much more comfortable for your little planner to take a rest at last . . . . You can relax now, you can surrender all challenges and obstacles, all the mental clutter that keeps you from the freedom meant to be yours.

And now, as the Tibetan chant guides, you rest in natural great peace . . . . This exhausted mind, beaten helplessly by karma and neurotic thoughts. Like the relentless fury of the pounding waves on the infinite Sea of Samsara . . . . Rest in natural great peace.

You are free, now . . . . You are a part of a Greater Intelligence which has absolutely no barriers, no limits, nothing that it cannot move or resolve creatively . . . . You let go your focus on lack, on your perception of what is missing or causing distress and fasten your focus on what is larger than these concerns . . . . You are reconnecting with resources that are coming your way more and more as you open your mind, as you soften your thoughts, as you create an atmosphere that is conducive to your complete relaxation, your complete sense of safety and reassurance . . . . And you find yourself breathing in and breathing out all that comforts and renews your faith in the Law of Creation flowing through you like a river, the River of Life.

And you rest in this natural great peace, allowing all thoughts of lack, all feelings of fear to just melt away like snowflakes on a warm windowpane . . . . Breathing in and breathing out kindness for yourself, for your Little Planner, knowing that even this aspect of your being is trying to help you in its own way.

And so, you thank this part of your mind that's been working way, way, way too hard . . . . Breathing in and out, you allow this Little Planner to take a long . . . . overdue rest . . . . To really rest now, in the Heart of Love. You continue breathing in and out down to the very core, the very essence of your being, your cells, where new life is being conceived with every new healthy thought . . . . Breathing in and out your own movement, your own growing . . . . softly noticing the footprints which have brought you to this moment . . . . You are cherishing the courage behind these many footprints . . . . your own courage . . . . the courage of those who've gone before you . . . . your people's people . . . . And you see that each of you were called into Life at the time that each was needed as a recording instrument, through which the Law of Creation, could express itself in unique and necessary ways to tell the human story.

You are breathing in and breathing out gratitude . . . deeply moving appreciation for the Rainmakers you've met, in all their forms. People you've known, but even strangers who, by example, have reminded you of what matters most to your heart. And you allow yourself to drift downward into your center even more, and as you do so, you sense an entire world within you. A Cosmos of which you are a part, and in which you reside, informing one another of all that wants to come to life... You are feeling this movement, this Dance of Life, of which you are a part. And you allow your heart to fill up and overflow with those desires, those wishes which bring you the deepest sense of aliveness . . . the deepest sense of joy. And you notice that very gently, way, way far back on the horizon of your creative imagination, there is an order forming something that brings you immense joy at the very prospect. And you are noticing that this very order connects you with a Higher Presence, an Eternal Substance whose sole purpose is to express your heart's desire through your life.

You are arriving at a place of deepest peace, where there is nothing whatsoever for you to do. Your only job is to receive in this present moment, to let this be your focus . . . your surrender . . . your true relationship with what is greater and more generous than you can imagine. From this place, you feel something within your deepest make-up that longs for fuller expression in your life . . . and it is good . . . and it comes from a Greater Good   and you are a reflection and child of this Greater Good . . . here, on Its behalf. And you are practicing certain things with greater, more truthful surrender than ever before. You are practicing in four ways. You are:

#1. Practicing focusing your awareness.

Notice your experience right now. What is it? Trust what comes. Surrendering to this greater good and to new life longing to grow through it. Breathing in and out, aligning with Creation, relaxing into a greater wisdom flowing through your heart's instincts.

#2. Practicing coming into true relations with all things.

Even the most challenging thing, which vanishes as you practice, turning your focus in healing directions. New life is returning through your breath. You are connecting with the bigger story, of which you are a part, giving and receiving nourishment within a larger tribe.

3. Practicing taking only true action that comes from love.

Doing only that which resonates with your heart, and bypassing the rest. Returning again and again to what lifts your Spirit and returns your joy . . . your gratitude.

#4. Sensing yourself practicing.

True surrender, *expressing your experience, in your own most naturally creative way*, what you discover, so that others are benefiting see it as so.

Prescription

Describe, in no more than two sentences per day, what "comes" to you in your surrender meditation using your journal or the pages in the back of this book. Date each day, including the year. You can avoid this exercise if you want. However, if you do it each day, you will receive the gold that that which is seeking you is attempting to offer you as a gift; your personal secret to getting more out of life!

Stepping out of the thinking and conceptual mind . . . does not mean stepping into nowhere or nothing, it does not mean that there is no connection to a worldly reality. We do not become disconnected or cast adrift. Rather, it is a stepping into sanity, and, more importantly, into even greater connectedness.

Jon Kabat-Zinn

I met Jon Kabit-Zinn many years ago at the Menninger Clinic in Kansas, where many of us gathered to explore our relationship to a connected, collaborative universe. What became clear to me then, once again, is the fact that we are hard-wired for collaborative loving action through our self-compassionate creative expression of this, each day.

What has become increasingly clear is that our best, most deeply satisfying experiences come only after we surrender to a sense of deeper belonging to the Universe. To arrive at this place, we must cast off our need to fit in or to be approved of, and set sail for wholehearted living, holding hands, together.

CHAPTER 58

Debriefing Surrender
to the Law of Creation

You and I can set goals. We know how to do this. We can achieve them if we are sincere and take consistent action in that direction. We can do our own thing, but, ultimately, after those achievements are put to bed, and we've acquired a certain skill set, something deeper in us knows there's more. Finding out what this is (which gets down to expressing more of who you really are) is part of the life you are building, informed by the silence of your heart. But the other is the realization that you cannot offer your richest contribution to others without awakening to the presence of connection to a greater good. Jung calls this "the Infinite." Creating this relationship shifts everything. Even when you are alone, you are never alone in the Stillness. A greater Life breathes Itself through you, to the degree you choose true surrender.

We are in a totally new game, so we need to find out the game rules and how to make the shift from the old to the new. How do you make this leap in your mind? It's an inside job. It's transforming your relationship with the greater self. The beginning of such a New Age is the death throes of the patriarchy. You must take heart, for as Clarissa Pinkola Estes points out: "We are mighty ships built for these times."

Your mighty ship is built for these times of inexplicable encounter. " . . . . a person removed from his own room almost without preparation and transition and set upon the height of a great mountain range, would feel something of the sort, an unparalleled insecurity, an abandonment to something inexpressible would almost annihilate him. He would think himself falling or hurled into space, or exploded into a thousand pieces: what a monstrous lie his brain would have to invent to catch up with and explain the state of his senses!...the only courage that is demanded of us; to have courage for the most singular, and the most inexplicable that we may encounter.

How Do You Find Courage for the Most Inexplicable Encounters?

I am reminded of meeting with returning veterans of war during the Vietnam war, and more recently, the Middle East. You and I both know the deployment brings many to the Edge of multiple traumas. I've held more than a few soldiers as they described the horror of seeing their buddies die from gunfire and unexpected explosions. I've heard stories that have made the hair on the back of my neck stand upright; scenes of women and children being killed, wounded as if they'd been hurled into the very bowels of hell. How do these soldiers go on?

While I do not have statistical numbers to report, I have witnessed enough stories to understand that in these overwhelming circumstances of trauma, what appears to be present is an experience of presence in the moment. In the presence, on the Edge between life and death, every (another word I've created) 'shribbon' of pretense, of cultural veneer, is stripped away. What remains is the naked, vulnerable pulse of life. It is palpable.

Paradoxically, in an atmosphere of chronic loss and chaos, there is a gratitude for life for connection, for camaraderie, and for humor (especially gallows humor). Within this "community," what emerges is a deepened sense of belonging. The individual feels necessary to the shared mission.

Imagine, if you will, the contrast they feel when they come home. Of course, their families suffer, profoundly, for their return is desperately needed. Without preparation or transition, each must face reunion with their invisible backpacks of trauma. Learning to reconnect, to share a sense of belonging and collaboration, is among the most difficult of all tasks. So, there is traumatic stress from what has happened, yes, but there is also distress from an interrupted thread of belonging and the identity bonding that comes from shared life and death experiences on precarious terrain with their buddies.

So, there you have it. The ingredient to your further development includes the necessity of addressing where you carry your own tension of opposites, which presents itself during times of disorientation. This is why it's so useful to contemplate not only the details of the life you'd most like to be living and write it down (yes, write it down), but you must also let yourself connect with the deepest feeling this would bring. Bringing this feeling forward into your life and placing your order. And when what your heart desires comes about, then prepare for another leap of growth. Prepare to meet others on their journey of encounter. Prepare to discover that even though your stories are different, you are not alone. Prepare to discover that your story goes on beyond your previous identity.

Prescription

Describe a time in your own life when you needed to go beyond your old identity, when you were in transition. Include what helped you most:

_____

_____

_____

_____

CHAPTER 59

Surrendering Ambition

Regardless of whether you've known war internally or externally, one thing is certain, if you are willing to be honest. When you've taken your biggest leaps of faith into the unknown, you've felt vulnerable and unclear about how to answer the most basic question.

I am reminded of this while sitting with the brave, day after day. Said one well-known attorney this morning, "I'm so stressed about going to this conference tomorrow, none of the guys I know have a clue that I'm sick of law. None of them know how stressful it's become to go on and on. None of them know I want to quit yet have no idea what my purpose is for what comes next. All I know is I want to feel better. I can't even say this because I'd be hit with so many questions and judgments. So, I'm walking around with this secret life. I don't want to be overly-exposed or dishonest. I'm between a rock and a hard place. My life as I've known it feels like it's over, and maybe I'll never even have success like I have, whatever that means."

He's not alone. I told him the following:

Build a chapel within your heart. At a certain, more advanced place in the creative process, the killing thing is ambition, the fear of what others will think if you reinvent yourself. This comes from your ego's power needs.

The saving thing is that which nourishes, delights, and serves your heart. Consider what top-selling author Elizabeth Gilbert said after she surrendered her old identity and found international fame, fortune, and even more important, the surrender of her heart to love:

> If your greatest success were behind you, how do you go on? The anguish comes if you believe that you did it, created it, and expressed this Mysterious thread through you.

Perhaps it helps to consider nature. If you've ever seen a forest fire, you know how devastating it can be. For a recent example, think Maui. The immediate aftermath is charred ruins, dense smoke, and death. And yet if you return years later, you discover the most amazing thing. New growth will sprout from fallen trees, filling the atmosphere with that sort of fresh green vitality that revitalizes you, as well.

Judge Troward amplifies this for us:

> The great fact to be realized regarding Nature is that it is natural, we may pervert the order of Nature, but it will prevail in the long run, returning . . . by the back door even though we drive it out with a pitchfork. . . . The law of Nature is the principle of growth from a vitality inherent in the entity itself . . . success depends (on) the greater vitality we put into the germ . . . .

We sabotage new life by rushing and running in circles fretting; by getting bogged down in apathy and indifference. If we don't care for new life, we mutate its growth.

The same thing applies to our children. Every week, when I was with my granddaughter, Talia Marie, born on New Year's Day in 2010, I find new life sprouting. The seed of new growth is planted in her every cell, every antic, every self-expression. Last time, as a newborn, she gazed with a wide open stare. Six months later she became "Turbo Crawler." Shortly thereafter, she walked around the room for the first time. She surrendered to the unseen, trusted the Law of Creation, and stepped into the unknown. Each day she reinvented herself, crossing new thresholds into greater possibility. So can you. We'd do well to follow suit. Today she stands on the threshold of fourteen this New Year's Day, with all the challenges this brings a teenager.

Apparently, our little ones know they want to move with greater freedom. They experiment. They fall. They get up again and begin anew. They are in a perpetual state of reinvention and identity revision. All they know is that where they are is more important than where they've been. They follow their instincts.

Following true feeling and your instincts is crucial. The idea is neither to minimize nor inflate ourselves, but rather, to come into more awakened, growing relationship with Creative Intelligence, and notice how it is pushing you toward self-compassion. Our thoughts give direction to the Universal Fund, there to serve the advancement of life. In itself, the Universal Fund is neutral on what It creates. Sowing seeds of doubt creates more doubt. Sowing seeds from surrender creates your most fruitful harvest. Watch the seeds you sow! They are beyond powerful, containing secret forces.

Prescription

Do NOT skip the following:

Experiment with saying to yourself: "Life force is flowing through me to create something beautiful . . . Life force is flowing through me to create something beautiful."

Do this daily for the next twenty-one days, especially when you get caught in tension. Record what happens in your journal or on the following pages.

After you've said the following several times, record your experience. "Life force is flowing through me, creating something beautiful . . ."

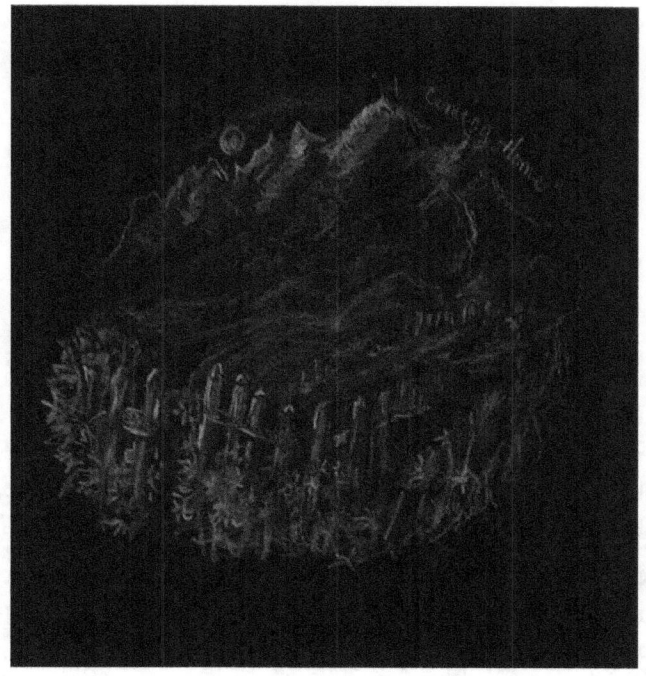

"Coming Home" Original painting (in color) by Cara Barker, 1995

Our journey through our lives is one of departure from the familiar, entry into the unfamiliar and mysterious, and return to a deeper truth which we are here to express. It is the eternal cycle of growth.

CHAPTER 60

Until We Meet Again

Some days are harder than other to do what we are here to do with joy in our hearts. Take this morning, for example. I met with my pre-operative team to get X-rays again, as well as a blood draw and EKG, all in anticipation of complete knee replacement. When I was told that I must take three months off post-op, my gut tightened. How am I supposed to do this? Still working, and with my husband in assisted living (which costs a bundle), I felt that surge of 'oh no' as my Spirit sunk. How quickly we can rev up into the need to control what cannot be controlled. It's futile. We human beings are so inclined to control people and outcomes that we cannot. Letting go is a necessary skill set if we are sincere about heart-led living.

I needed to loosen my grip on what cannot be controlled. Blessedly, I remember you and our time together. It helped me to, as they say, 'get a grip.' The question I asked myself was this: what if this is *for me?* The answer came right away. Knowing for some time I needed a rest break, something always seemed to get in the way.

Recall the construction workers I met at the beginning of this book? Recall that Juan told me that digging down is tricky. He said, "You never know what will be in the way: gas lines, power lines . . ." to which he added the story of the man who did a deep dig that was necessary to build a firm foundation. And what did that guy find impeding his way? Yes, a dirty diaper, but also a diamond.

Recalling his tale, I am free to ask myself how I want to frame this three-month hiatus: a dirty diaper experience (not literally), or one which might reveal the diamond? I invite you to do the same when you hit the unexpected, apparent setbacks while building the best heart-led life you can.

We always have choice. Heart-led living requires that we remember we do have a choice regarding the perspective we choose. As for me, what I choose to next embark upon will be a surprise.

Nature's Teachers

Just now, a robin flew by my window. Is she worried? Confused? More like she is fully engaged in spreading her wings. Let's follow her example and spread our wings today, ride the currents, and open our hearts and minds to something more beautiful than we can imagine. Arrive.

We are never alone. Yes, we might feel lonely for a bit. One thing I know for certain is that there are invisible forces at work behind everything that happens. Let's embrace our empty hands by trusting that only when we empty ourselves of our limiting beliefs, our prejudices, our fears, and the attempt to control what cannot be controlled can something beautiful arrive. As my friend Nancy Simpson told me over fifty years ago, an hour before she died, "No matter how hard winter has been, spring always comes again."

When you catch yourself in self-doubt, self-criticism, and frustration, when you feel like you've gotten "stuck," my hope is that the following tips I've discovered along the way might be useful to move forward! Godspeed.

Realizations at My Edge:

1. Forgive continuously, beginning with yourself.

2. It's okay to start over.

3. Making a mess is not only the end of the world, but it can also be the beginning of a better one!

4. Striving for perfection is a waste of energy and resources.

5. Since you can't do it all, do the one thing that delights your heart first.

6. We are all doing the best we can.

7. I'm not for everyone.

8. And, that's okay.

9. A day without laughter is a day not fully lived.

10. My Spirit and my instincts have an infallible wisdom.

11. I can only locate myself inside.

12. It's okay to choose fun.

13. We can create nothing of lasting value alone.

14. The end brings us to new beginnings.

You are always in my heart.

OTHER BOOKS AND ARTICLES
BY CARA LEE BARKER, Ph.D

Nightlight: My Soul Calling, Body Listening, Heart Speaking
Best Seller Publishing, 2022

World Wearly Woman: Her Wound and Transformation.
Published by Inner City, Toronto, 2001

The Love Project
Published by University Press, 2012

Huffington Post Archives; GPS for the Soul

Grieving the Loss of Your Child
Sounds True Studio

References

Barker, Cara. *Coming Home to Yourself.* The Motherhouse, 2010. CD.

Barker, Cara. *Grieving the Loss of a Child.* Boulder: Sounds True, 1992.

Barker, Cara. "Healthy Living." New York: The Huffington Post, Archives (weekly) 2007-2011.

Barker, Cara. *Practicing Love.* Seattle: The Motherhouse, 2010. CD.

Barker, Cara. *World Weary Woman: Her Wound and Transformation.* Toronto: Inner City Publishers, 2001.

Barker, Cara. *Reclaiming the Feminine Authority.* Boulder: Sounds True, 1986.

Bateson, Mary Catherine. *Willing to Learn: Passages of Personal Discovery.* Hanover, CT: Steerforth, 2004.

Bridges, William. *Managing Transitions: Making the Most of Change Reading,* pp.3-6. Reading, MA: Addison-Wesley, 1991

Perugia, Luciano. *Brother Sun, Sister Moon.* Paramount Pictures, 1972. Film.

Browning, Elizabeth Barrett. *Complete poetical works of Elizabeth Barrett Browning.* BiblioLife, SC, 2009.

Chodron, Pema. "Becoming Pema." *Shambala Sun*, November 2009.

Chodron, Pema. "When Things Fall Apart: Heart Advice for Difficult Times." *Shambala Sun*, January 2002.

Cox, Carol Thayer, and Peggy Osna Heller. *Portrait of the artist as poet*. Chicago, IL: Magnolia Street Publishers, 2006.

De, Castilleuo Irene Claremont. *Knowing woman*. London, England: Hodder, 1973.

Eckhart, Meister, Bernard McGinn, and Edmund Colledge. *The essential sermons, commentaries, treatises, and Defense*. New York, NY: Paulist Press, 1981.

Edinger, Edward Ferdinand. *Encounter with the self: A Jungian commentary on William Blake's illustrations of The book of job*. Toronto, Canada: Inner city Books, 1986.

Edwards, Phillip. *Hamlet, Prince of Denmark*. Cambridge: Cambridge University Press, 1985.

Eldridge, John. *Desire: The Journey We Must Take to Find the Life God Offers*, pp. 7, 191. Nashville: Thomas Nelson, 2007.

Eliade, Mircea. *The Sacred and the Profane: The Nature of Religion* (trans. By Willard R. Trask). New York: Harper Touchbooks, 1961.

Eliot, T. S.. *Four Quartets*. San Diego: Harcourt, Brace and Co., 1943.

Estes, Clarissa P. *Women Who Run With the Wolves*. New York: Ballantine Books, 1992.

Frankl, Viktor. *Man's Search for Meaning*. New York: Buccaneer Books, 1993.

Frost, Robert. *Mountain Interval*. New York: Henry Holt, 1920. Print.

Gaines, Edwene. "Leap of Faith: Meet John of God." *Oprah Magazine*, December 2010: 22. Print.

Gilbert, Elizabeth. "Your Elusive Creative Genius." YouTube, February 9, 2009. http://www.youtube.com/watch?v=86x-u-tz0MA.

Gladwell, Malcolm. *Outliers: the Story of Success*. New York: Little, Brown and Company, 2008.

Guinness, Os. *The Call: Finding and Fulfilling the Central Purpose of Your Life*, p. 42. Nashville: Thomas Nelson, 1998.

Holmes, Ernest). *This Thing Called You*. Los Angeles: Tarcher, 2007.

Hopkins, Emma Curtis. *Scientific Christian Mental Practice*, p. 240. New York: Cosimo, 1888.

Jung, Carl. *The Red Book*, p.232. New York: W.W. Norton & Company, 2009.

Jung, Carl. *Memories, Dreams, Reflections*. New York: Vintage Books, 1989.

Jung, Carl. *Mysterium Coniunctionis*. London: Routledge, 1963.

Keating, Father Thomas. *Open Mind, Open Heart*. New York: Continuum, 2006.

Khenpo, Nyoshul. *A Marvelous Garland of Rare Gems: Biographies of Masters of Awareness in the Dzogchen Lineage*. Junction City, CA: Padma Publications, 2005.

Kidd, Sue Monk. *When the Heart Waits*, pp. 7, 69. New York: HarperCollins Publishers, 1980.

Kirshenbaum, Mira. *The Gift of a Year*. New York: Penguin Group, 2000.

Lamont, Anne. "Becoming the Person you Were Meant to Be: Where to Start," *Oprah Magazine* November 2009: 18. Print.

Lawrence-Lightfoot, Sara. *The Third Chapter: Passion, Risk, and*

Adventure in the 25 Years After 50, p. 33, 172. London: Macmillan, 2009.

Len, Ihaleakala Hew. *Zero Limits*, p. 62. Hoboken, NJ: John Wiley & Sons, Inc., 2007.

Lewis, C. S. *The Great Divorce*. New York: HarperCollins Publishers, 1946.

Lewis, C. S. *A Grief Observed*. New York: HarperCollins Publishers, 1961.

Lindberg, Anne Morrow. *Gifts From the Sea*, pp. 17, 51, 127-128. New York: Knopf Publishing Group, 1986.

Logue, Christopher. *New Numbers*, pp. 65-66. London: Cape, 1969.

Madison, Ed (Director). Barker, Cara (Speaker). "The Answer to Absolutely Everything."
Engaging Media, 2008. DVD.

Malachi, Tau. *The Gnostic Gospel of St. Thomas*. Woodbury, MN: Llewellyn Publications, 2004.

Maxwell, John C. *The Choice is Yours*. Nashville: Thomas Nelson, 2005.

Mehl-Madrona, Lewis. *Narrative Medicine*, pp.17-18. Rochester, VT: Bear and Co., 2007.

Murray, William Hutchinson. *The Scottish Himalayan Expedition*. London: J.M. Dent and Sons, 1951.

Oliver, Mary. *Wild Geese*. Northumberland, UK: Bloodaxe Books Ltd., 2004.

Quinn, Robert. *Change the World: How Ordinary People Can Achieve Extraordinary Results*, p.136. New York: John Wiley & Sons, 2000.

Rilke, Rainier Maria. *Letters to a Young Poet*. New York: W.W. Norton, 1934.

Shapiro, Ed and Deb. *Be the Change: How Meditation Can Transform You and the World*. New York: Sterling Ethos, 2009.

Taylor, Susan L. *Lessons in Living*, pp. 7, 9, 20, 64. New York: Anchor Books, 1998.

Troward, Thomas. *The Creative Process in the Individual*. Gloucester: Dodo Press, 2008.

Troward, Thomas. *The Edinburgh and Dore Lectures on Mental Science*, p. 17.

Camarillo, CA: De Vorss and Co. Pub., 1909.

van der Post, Laurens. *The Hunter and the Whale*, Ch. 12. New York: William Morrow & Company, Inc., 1967

van der Post, Laurens. *Jung and the Story of Our Time*. New York: Pantheon Books, 1975.

Whyte, David. *The House of Belonging*. Langley, WA: Many Rivers Press, 1997.

Williamson, Marianne. *The Gift of Change: Spiritual Guidance for Living Your Best Life* p. 12. New York: HarperOne, 2004.

The New Jerusalem Bible. Ed. Susan Jones. New York: Doubleday, 1985. Print.

Acknowledgements

None of what follows would have happened without a mighty big dose of "miago." I love this word. Whenever Ecuadorians utter the word, there is immediate recognition. Everyone drops whatever they are doing and runs to wherever they must to assist one another. Very simply, "miago" means "we come together for the common good."

If our world is ever to advance in the direction of a Greater Good, and to live out a more beautiful dream here on Earth, it is up to us to sound the all "miago" and to respond when we hear it. The events of recent days and decades make one thing clear: our remedy lies in connection, in outreach, and in lending a hand to whoever seeks help, for we are brothers and sisters in a larger family than just that of our bloodline. Thich Nhat Hahn refers to this as "interbeing." Another word for this is "umbutu." It means: "I am because we are."

The secret of getting more out of life has a great deal to do with these ways of "languaging" what is vital to our evolution into more compassion, kindness, generosity, and patience for ourselves as well as others. What we are talking about here is nothing less than Soul Consciousness.

So much of what is contained in the pages before you came about because at the core level of the heart, there have been those who sounded the call "miago," and I heard them. There have been many such cries, although it took many years for me to piece together what form the answer to their plea might take. As the material began to take shape, I was reminded that I am a card-carrying member of "umbutu." While my name might be assigned as "author," the fact is that Truth has no author. It has been my greatest honor to hear the stories of others as it pertains to this Love Project, and to offer it here as but one means of supporting the awakening of our planet, beginning with our own journey home through fear to freedom.

For those who have gone before, I am most grateful to you for your profound teachings, who include, but are not limited to: Helen Luke, Carl Jung, my son Matt, Anne Morrow Lindberg, poets Hafiz and Rumi, C.S. Lewis, Victor Frankl, Ellie Wiesel, Elisabeth Kubler-Ross, Hermann Strobel, Carrie Majors, Meister Eckhart, the Master Jesus, Buddha, Kwan Yin, Sophia, Emma Curtis Hopkins, Eric Butterworth, Howard Thurman, Charles and Myrtle Fillmore, Ernest Holmes, Esther Harding, John Eldridge, Susan L. Taylor, Irene de Castillejo, Barbara Hannah, Catherine Bateson, Sara Lawrence-Lightfoot, Andriette Earl, Kathianne Lewis, Jim Munson, Michael Beckweth, and Pema Chodron.

I am grateful, as well, to friends and colleagues who offered inspiration, ideas, support, and suggestions, as well as input, to my process of writing, especially Vicki Heland, Bridget Agabra, Callie Sheehan, Jane Meyers-Bowen, Dr. Jenny Gordon, Dr. Sylvia Weishaupt, Mary Oliver, and Marion Woodman, and especially Sylvia Weishaupt and Len and Teresa Marcel.

For my midwives over the years, and in particular Vicki Heland, Kitty Farmer, Hannelore Hahn, and Bridget Agabra. What can I say? Your devotion, good cheer, and belief in the imperative of love alive in the world as the ultimate project. You have all been a resting place for trust to come again.

About the Author

Dr. Cara Barker is an author, artist, and Jungian Analyst. A featured contributor for the *Huffington Post* through a weekly column called "GPS for the Soul," Cara's delight is in the discovery of the story beneath the story of transformation. An evolutionary agent in the life of others, Barker helps them to liberate their unlived life and awaken what has grown dry through activating the neuroplasticity of the brain. One might say she is a map maker and practical visionary for that audience seeking to be free. A popular guest speaker around the world, she devotes her life to assisting those who are committed to achieving greater aliveness through their daily experience and contribution.

With the Soul of an artist, she is devoted to the creative act of transforming the human story and teaching how to cultivate the best conditions for profound reconnection and healing for the human heart. Currently, she is focusing considerable creative talents in the direction of children and adults around the world who desire to learn the secret of living more joy-filled lives through acts of recognition, Love Projects, and customized celebrations of life for those we love. She is the author of multiple publications, which include *World Weary Woman: Her Wound and Transformation, Grieving the Loss of a Child, Reclaiming Your Feminine Authority*, and *Nightlight: My Soul Calling, Body Listening, Heart Speaking*, and was a featured contributor in *The Artist as Poet* and *The Last Time I Said Goodbye to My Mother*. She may be reached at carabarker.com

"What Cara Barker brings to the field of depth psychology is both inspirational and practical. She is that rare combination of artist, healer, and teacher, with a full grasp of the process of truly drawing from the depths what is imperative to create healing. Hers is a major contribution to the art of healing."

Gene D. Cohen, M.D., PH.D., NIH Director for the Department on Aging, Director of the Center on Aging, Health, and Humanities at George Washington University, founding director of the Washington, D.C., Center on Aging, and author of *The Mature Mind* and *The Creative Age*.

www.ingramcontent.com/pod-product-compliance
Lightning Source LLC
Chambersburg PA
CBHW071137130626
46553CB00004B/1412